SURPRISED BY GOD

SURPRISED BY GOD

How and Why What We Think about the Divine Matters

Chris E. W. Green

CASCADE *Books* · Eugene, Oregon

SURPRISED BY GOD
How and Why What We Think about the Divine Matters

Cascade Books
An Imprint of Wipf and Stock Publishers
199 W. 8th Ave., Suite 3
Eugene, OR 97401

www.wipfandstock.com

PAPERBACK ISBN: 978-1-5326-3565-6
HARDCOVER ISBN: 978-1-5326-3567-0
EBOOK ISBN: 978-1-5326-3566-3

Cataloguing-in-Publication data:

Names: Green, Chris E. W., author.

Title: Surprised by God : how and why what we think about the divine matters /
Chris E. W. Green.

Description: Eugene, OR: Cascade Books, 2018 | Includes bibliographical refer-
ences.

Identifiers: ISBN 978-1-5326-3565-6 (paperback) | ISBN 978-1-5326-3567-0
(hardcover) | ISBN 978-1-5326-3566-3 (ebook)

Subjects: LCSH: God (Christianity) | Contemplation | Theology, Practical |
Spiritual life—Christianity

Classification: BT102 G72 2018 (paperback) | BT102 (ebook)

The Banjo Lesson by Henry Ossawa (1893) (p. 68) and *The Vulture and the
Little Girl* by Kevin Carter (1993) (p. 43) are in the public domain.
Christ and the Breadlines by Fritz Eichenberg (1953) (p. 61).
Christ Sending Forth the Disciples by David Jones (1924) (p. 62) permission
given by the Trustees of the David Jones Estate.
The Christ of the Breadlines by Franz Eichenberg (1955) (p. 61) copyright:
Estate of Fritz Eichenberg/Licensed by VAGA, New York, NY.

Manufactured in the U.S.A.   07/06/18

Contents

Preface

I had a very good reason for writing this book: my wife Julie told me to do it. Of course, even with her encouragement, the work proved difficult—and not only because of the normal difficulties of writing and editing. There are always troubles sufficient for every season. So, as I was writing, my maternal grandfather and grandmother, with whom I have always been close, passed away. And I struggled with a series of illnesses. Through it all, however, the effort has been if nothing else an opening of myself to healing. It has been good for me to think and pray through these words; perhaps that is why Julie pressed me to write it.

Saying it has been good for me to write this book is another way of saying that God has surprised me, again and again. I was raised to think of God in specific terms and to expect God to acts in particular ways. Now, most if not all of those terms and ways are lost to me. But only because God always proves to be more than those concepts and expectations can handle. Even if I am not always pleased to find this happening to me, I am happy that God is beyond all I ask or think.

Finally, I need to give thanks to those who helped make this writing possible. Thanks, first, to Julie and my children: Zoë, Clive, and Emery. They were not only patient but also relentlessly encouraging in making time for me to write and praying for me to do it well. Special thanks too for all the friends who read and responded to early drafts of these chapters: Hannah Moore, Dusty Counts, Ed Gungor, Mark Aarstad, and Adam Palmer. Without their readiness to take time to read and respond to my work, I would have had a very difficult time discerning what I needed to change or leave alone, what I should add or take away. Their friendship during this time has been a grace, and I am deeply grateful for it.

CHAPTER ONE

What to Do When the World Is on Fire

"There is no fear in love."

1 JOHN 4:18

"We only live, only suspire
Consumed by either fire or fire."

—T. S. ELIOT

Christians are called to live Christ's life in this world, embodying the fullness of his love. And that means we're called to live fearlessly. Now, we can all find much to be afraid of; at least we could if we lived by sight and not by faith. What Teresa of Avila said of her own age is true of ours (and all other ages) as well: the world is on fire; God seems to have so few friends and so many enemies. But fear is not a Christian affection. As St John reveals, the love of God has no fear in it, and deep-seated fears suffocate our ability to live lovingly with our neighbors (1 John 4:18). The fear of judgment, in particular, keeps us from being gracefully present to those most in need. Somehow, then, we must be delivered into fearlessness by the love of God.

At birth, we are hurled into trouble. There are evils sufficient for every day and terrors sufficient for every age. We know fear from the earliest beginnings of our lives, long before we are capable of gratitude or humility, wonder or awe. In the words of Job, "mortals, born of woman, are of few days and full of trouble." So how can we possibly live fearlessly? Given the state of things in this world, doesn't even the desire to live without fear mean we are either naively selfish, concerned only with our own safety and comfort, or foolishly selfless, ready to put ourselves and our neighbors through unnecessary, meaningless suffering?

We have to find a way to move toward fearlessness—without deceiving ourselves. But how? We have to allow ourselves to be shown a reality truer than our experiences. Like Teresa, we have to look away from the world to God for the world's sake. In times of crisis, we need to turn aside to God as Moses did, averting our gaze from all illusions of mastery and control, as well as from all specters of futility and meaninglessness, fixing our attention on the God revealed in the gospel. As Maximus Confessor reminds us, human life is lived in the shadow of death; only if we know the God who lives with us can we rightly pass through the valley of the shadow of death without dread of the evils. Fear is a way of apprehending reality, a way of receiving the world, and only by looking to God instead of the world can we be freed from it. To that end, we have to learn contemplation.

***

We are already familiar with God. At least many of us are day in and day out saturated with Christian images and sounds. We easily recognize descriptions of the divine nature (God is one, holy, good, omniscient, omnipotent, omnipresent). We are sure we know how to call on God, and we are quick to profess our confidence in him and desire for him. But if we want really to be freed to live the lives we're called to live, lives authentically devoted to doing justice, loving mercy, and walking humbly before God, we have to penetrate the veil of that familiarity, pressing toward a transfiguring vision of God as he is revealed to us. It is not enough to know the divine names or to have a felt sense of the divine presence. We need to grasp—or, better, be grasped by—a vision of the divine nature and character. We have to come to know as fully as possible with life-determining force what God is really like.

But how is it possible for us, as the finite, broken creatures we are, to know what God is really like? Even our own wisdom is incomprehensible to us; how much more God's wisdom? Thomas Aquinas can help us here. In this life, he insists, we cannot know what God *in himself* is like, not even by the grace of faith. Until our transformation with all things at the end of history, there remains between God and us such an absolute difference that we simply are not capable of knowing God as he essentially is. But Thomas is quick to add that this does not mean God cannot be known now in *any* sense. God by nature is supremely knowable, and because he is good, he desires to be known by creatures in ways fitted to the reality purposed for us. In fact, it is precisely the mode of our knowledge of God that makes us what we are. As we are being made capable of knowing who and what he is, he is transforming who and what we are so that we are brought into the fullness of the purpose given to us from the foundation of all things.

Given that the above is true, we can perhaps identify three such modes of knowing. First, there is the knowledge of God that comes naturally to us, which is something like an intuitive, existential sense of our creatureliness, a fractured awareness of being in relation to an absolute and mysterious otherness. From time to time in the course of our daily lives, we become aware of the fact that we are answerable to this mystery that lies at the limits of our existence. At other times, we sense, however vaguely, what Simone Weil's describes as a "longing for an absolute good . . . a longing which is always there and is never appeased by any object in this world." That's not to say that every one of us thinks about that longing and recognizes it for what it is. But it is to say that we know God in some sense just by experiencing that longing, however we name it.

Second, there is the knowledge of God given by grace through faith, which teaches us to identify God rightly, selecting him out from all the so-called gods as the true and living one. By the Spirit's gift of faith and Christ's patient presence to us, we come over time more and more fully to adore God's nature and to trust his character. This graced, faithful knowledge is both intellectual and affective, doctrinal and experiential. It fulfills the longing created by our natural knowing of God as in secret, hidden ways it also takes us out beyond the sheerly intellectual or affective, effecting a kind of stilling or silencing of our thoughts and feelings in communion with God.

Finally, there is the knowledge of God given in the final transformation of all things. In that moment, according to Aquinas, God unites himself to us and us to himself so that we come to know God as we are known by God. We see God as he is, and in this way become like him. It is only the work of the Father as witness to Christ that moves us from the first to the second mode of knowing God. In the same way, it is only the appearing of Christ, which is the Spirit's fulfillment of history, that moves us from the second to the third. In the fullness of time, we move from the glory of image to the glory of likeness, from the glory of faith to the glory of sight.

***

To reiterate: so long as we live by sight and not by faith, we will be troubled with fears of all kinds, real and imagined. And so long as we are troubled by those fears, we will remain incapable of loving our neighbors freeingly or faithfully. If we believe we are responsible to manage our own futures, if we feel we can and should control what happens to us and to those around us, if we remain at the mercy of our own passions and the pressures of the powers of this age, then we are sure to live—and to cause others to live—from terror to terror and not from grace to grace. So, in this time before the fullness of times, only contemplation frees us for worldly living.

But perhaps I've still not quite made clear what it means to contemplate God. It means, as Rowan Williams has said, "to look to God without regard to my own instant satisfaction." It means allowing God to be God for me, making room for "the prayer of Christ, God's own relation to God, to come alive in me" so that I am opened up compassionately to my neighbor. In contemplation, the Holy Spirit broods sweetly over my spirit, slowly and secretly freeing me from "slavery to cravings and fantasies," making me permeable to Christ so that his character begins to alter mine, filling me with the goodness of his own Spirit—joy and peace, gentleness and self-control. In contemplation, in other words, we open ourselves up to the sanctifying work of God, a work that takes time and happens almost entirely below the level of our conscious awareness. In Joseph Pieper's phrase, contemplation is "a knowing which is inspired by love," a knowing that God creates in us just as we give ourselves, heart and mind and soul, to considering God as he is and all things as they are in him.

How does this knowing happen in us? What part do we play in its happening? Is there a way that we can intentionalize our participation? How do we yield to the Spirit? Above all, we attend to the revelation of God given in the Scriptures and the church's reading and performance of those Scriptures until our attention becomes a kind of ceaseless prayer, until the communion that is God's own life as Trinity begins to happen among and between us—in ways we can see and ways we cannot see. As we are attending habitually to who God is, faithful attention begins to come alive in us. And just as our lives are being opened to God's, we can trust that we are being delivered from the fear that dehumanizes us and thwarts our vocation.

We will not be delivered from it all at once, of course. And no doubt our expectations will be disappointed again and again. But if the church has witnessed faithfully to the character and nature of God, then we can be sure that as we allow God's own relation to God to happen in us, our humanity, our creatureliness, will be renewed so that we can care for others without oppressing them. This is the heart of the matter: nothing is as humanizing, as sanctifying, as contemplating the beauty of God and the glory he shares with our neighbor.

***

Contemplation is not just one kind of thing Christians do. It is, instead, basic to everything we do. Of course, silent, contemplative prayer is at the heart of the contemplative life, and we all would do well to practice it. But contemplation is not reducible to a form of regular, meditative prayer any more than it is simply identical with theological reflection. Instead, contemplation is a mode of orientation to life, a manner of engaging and receiving reality, a way of apprehending as gift everything that comes to us. Contemplation is attentional living. It is attending to God in all things, at all times, and to all things, at all times, in God.

If we hope to live this kind of life, attentive to God in the midst of our worldly experiences, we need to learn as well as we can the revealed truth about the divine nature and character. Of course, contemplation cannot be reduced to the ideas we have about God. It should go without saying that the goal is not merely to hold orthodox opinions, whatever that might mean. But contemplation *is* inseparably bound up with the ways we think of God, even if it remains distinct from our thinking about God and finally transcends it altogether. Our worship and our witness, our speaking to God and for God with and for one another, our participation in God's work in the world, depend at every point on faithful teaching and learning of the truth about who God is and what he is like.

To be sure, there is a knowing of God that exceeds anything we can think or feel about God. But movement out into the divine mystery runs along the way opened up by doctrine, and by the constant consideration of the nature and character of God. Our convictions about God matter. And these convictions cannot truly be ours, cannot be integrated transformingly into our lives, apart from shared reflection on what it is that we think about God as we are attempting to perform the gospel. The more our beliefs about God come into line with the truth, the more available we make ourselves for the deep transformation necessary to see everything transfigured in the light of the character of the divine life.

All that said, we cannot forget that contemplation is always only gift and never an achievement. It happens always only as God freely awakens us to God. As Thomas Merton says in his book on contemplative prayer, "True contemplation is not a psychological trick but a theological grace. It can come to us only as a gift, and not as a result of our own clever use of spiritual techniques." The living God cannot be controlled or directed. The fire must fall on the altar; we cannot summon it. We can and should, however, posture ourselves for the awakening God has promised. In fact, that's how we know contemplation is beginning to take shape: we find ourselves being opened up to the happening of God in us, being brought slowly but truly into alignment with God's love of God and God's love of us, coming to know as we are known, becoming transparent to Christ as he has made himself transparent himself to us. We can and should, then, again and again ask ourselves why we love God and what it is in God that we find lovely, because in asking those questions we keep ourselves open to the possibility of answers that can surprise us, answers that can help us know how best to yield to God's work in our lives.

***

This way of looking to God in the midst of our lived experience of the world may not come easily, because many of us remain enslaved to the "practical." We've been trained to expect—and so to demand—truths that make instant, easy sense for us, truths that in some way immediately improve the quality of our lives. But as St. Augustine told us long ago, humans aren't just for using things. We are meant to enjoy God and neighbor, and to find ourselves through losing ourselves in God's enjoyment of our neighbor.

Contemplation of the divine nature and character, then, is a form of rebellion against the tyranny of the practical, and precisely in that way it is a refusal to live fearfully. Contemplation moves us beyond thinking of God as useful, as if he were a resource we draw on to make our lives what we have been told they should be. It reminds us that we are meant for more than getting things done and having things done to us. St. Thomas Aquinas described salvation as basically nothing more or less than reflecting on the divine essence now and always. If that doesn't sound very appealing, it's because we don't yet understand as we're meant to understand how beautiful and beautifying this God really is.

***

To be awakened by the Spirit to contemplation is not to live with a lasting sense of God's presence, or to enjoy constant consolation and peace. From time to time, we may find ourselves newly conscious of a deep, intimate communion with the love who is our life. But that is never what matters most. What matters most is that as we are living contemplatively we will begin to come newly aware of our *neighbors*, recognizing for the first time their true glory in their utter frailty. We will slowly come aware of the endless possibilities of caring for them so they can know the joy they're meant to know. Contemplation is in the end a way of loving our neighbors precisely because it is a way of loving and being loved by God.

Contemplation does not make us indifferent to evil or injustice. And contemplation does not solve all of our problems, or afford us everything we imagine we need. We do not turn to God so that in that experience we can find solace for or protection from the sorrows of this life. We do not pray, hidden away in spiritual ecstasies, while the world burns. Even as we keep our eyes on what cannot be seen, we, like everyone and everything else, suffer and die. Contemplation is nothing more or less than a way of living with God for our neighbors' sake, especially the neighbors who see themselves as our remove period the midst of this life we have been given to share with them. It is a mode of engaging the world in all of its brokenness as it is transfigured by the light of the hope we have in the goodness of God.

Seeing God as he is revealed in the life and death of Jesus Christ, to "look full in his wonderful face," is not to lose sight of the world but to see it rightly for the first time. Attunement to that reality is the only way to refuse to be dominated by the terrors of fear. Not that the world is somehow rendered safe for us by our delight in the beauty of God. Not in the least. But we are in truth transformed by our vision of that beauty into the likeness of Christ, made to share in the character of the one whom we are contemplating. Beholding God by faith enlightens the eyes of our heart so that we see reality differently, and just in this way it begins to free us from the fear that would keep us from being ourselves for one another. Filled up with the love of God, we are strengthened to live as Christ lives, giving ourselves fearlessly with him for the life of the world.

CHAPTER TWO

How (Not) to Believe in God

"The God who made the world and everything in it . . . does not live in shrines made by human hands, nor is he served by human hands, as though he needed anything."

Acts 17:24–25

"God is not a human being . . . ."

Numbers 23:19

"Our idea of God tells us more about ourselves than about Him."

THOMAS MERTON

We are terribly familiar with God—at least with talk about God. Many of us are so familiar, in fact, we rarely if ever stop to think what we mean by it or what it means for us. Unlike the Athenians Paul encountered on the Areopagus, we do know the name of the God we worship (Acts 17:16–34). But too often we have only a fragmented and obscured sense of his character and nature. We have been so obsessed with the mechanics of living the Christian life, focusing our attention on the demands of ministry and the dynamics of spiritual experience, that we've lost touch with who it is we call by this name "God" and how we are to speak rightly to him and about him. We are not "fools" who believe there is no God (Ps 14:1), but we somehow have been fooled into assuming that it doesn't matter much what we think about the God we are convinced we believe in. We know just enough not to realize how little we understand or why our ignorance and foolishness matter. In a strangely bitter twist, our very familiarity leaves us estranged.

As a result, our current situation is in at least one respect even more challenging than Paul's was. He had to explain the truth of God to people who readily admitted that they didn't yet know. We have to rediscover the truth of a God we mistakenly presume to understand. That means that at least for many of us the process of coming to know how to think and speak about God will be inseparably bound up with unlearning deeply-ingrained opinions about him. The deepest assumptions we've held about the divine nature and character must somehow be uprooted and torn down before we can give ourselves fully to the process of learning to think faithfully about God. Meister Eckhart's prayer has to become ours: *God (as you really are) rid us of God (as we imagine you to be).*

***

Many of our traditions have for a long time feared nothing quite so much as dead orthodoxy, lifeless spirituality, and ineffective religion. We've been convinced that what matters most is for our churches and ministries to get as many people as possible to believe as quickly as possible, and for individual believers to take responsibility for their "personal relationship with God" (rarely if ever stopping to consider what such language actually means). We've acted as if slow, deep catechesis is not terribly important, much less essential, in the discipleship process. And insofar as we give any attention to doctrine and theological formation at all, we've tended to focus on the distinctive teachings of our movement or denomination. Now, due as much to our successes as our failures, we are threatened not by *nominal* Christianities but by *false* ones. This comes particularly clear in what we say and think, explicitly and implicitly, directly and indirectly, about God. David Bentley Hart's diagnosis is right on point: our very concept of God has become "thoroughly impoverished, thoroughly mythical."

***

What is it that has gone so wrong in our thinking about God? And why does it matter? For many of us, whether we realize it or not, "God" refers to whatever it is that makes happen what we can't otherwise explain. God is one—the primary one, to be sure, but still just one—of the causes of things that happen in the world. And because we imagine God as one agent among others, we have to conclude that God must be sometimes present, sometimes absent, sometimes active, sometimes passive—often if not always in response to something we personally have done or failed to do. We remain convinced that God possesses the strength to overcome every possible resistance to his will, of course. He has more power than any other agent in the universe, more power than all other agents combined. But sometimes for reasons we can't quite decipher, God chooses not to overcome those resistances, leaving us to suffer the fallout from our own actions or the actions of others. Through it all, however, we do all that we can as people of faith to go on trusting that whatever God allows to happen will turn out for our good, somehow fitting into his plan for us.

Obviously, I think more or less everything in the view I've just sketched is mistaken in one way or another. But even if I'm right, so what? What difference does it make if what we think about the divine nature is misguided or misleading? Doesn't everything we say about God fail in the end to name the truth of the divine mystery? Theologians have always insisted that our understanding is no match for the divine reality. "If you think you have grasped God it is not God who you have grasped." "God is revealed precisely where creaturely understanding cannot reach." The lives of the saints impress on us the realization that there's a lot that happens to us spiritually that doesn't come as a direct result of theological study or reflection on the divine nature and character. And truth be told, no one with even the slightest sense of the complexity of our lives in the world could ever suggest there's any simple, linear relationship between theology and sanctification, between thinking about God and coming to share in his character. How can I argue, then, that how we think about God makes such a crucial difference?

I make the argument because I am convinced that we human beings are meant for the work of interpretation, created to make meaning of the reality given to us, purposed to know God in all things and all things in God. With that in mind, we can readily admit that all our thoughts about God are creaturely. Yes, our thinking and speaking fail to do what we wish they could do. Yes, reflection on the character and nature of God is highly demanding and at times even risky work. But this is nonetheless work that needs doing, work that belongs to the Spirit's shaping of our lives into the image of God in Christ. And to say that our words and thoughts are creaturely is not the same as saying they're worthless or vain. Just the opposite, in fact.

Hilary of Poitiers is unquestionably right to say that "our nature is not such that it can lift itself by its own forces to the contemplation of heavenly things. We must learn from God what we are to think of God; we have no source of knowledge but himself." But the faith delivered to us insists that God in fact *has* made himself known. We are learning from God what we are to think of God. We have not been left as orphans. As Kate Sonderegger has put it, God is so humble that he joyfully lays himself down in the embrace of our knowledge. In St. Paul's words, through the grace of the triune God, as the Spirit opens us up to the fullness of the life of the Son and the Son opens up to the fullness of the life of the Father, we come to know Christ with a knowledge that exceeds knowing. God just in this way raises us up beyond ourselves, beyond our own natural capacities and desires into the heights and depths, breadth and lengths of the divine mystery. This is the knowing of contemplation.

Theologically, we are led into this mystery primarily by the way of negation. We can know who and what God is only by recognizing who and what he is *not*. And that means learning to think faithfully about God is basic to discipleship and our formation into godli(ke)ness. (To be clear, learning to think about God is not the only lesson we have to learn—far from it; but it's a crucial lesson, nonetheless.) As Aquinas insists, "no name belongs to God in the same sense that it belongs to creatures." (For example, we may be wise, but God is not: God is God's own wisdom. We may be loving, but God is not: God is love itself.) The recognition that God is God comes to have force for us just as we are forced to reflect on what we are thinking and saying about God and what we mean when we think and say it. To that end, Edith Stein, the Jewish Catholic philosopher and Carmelite nun, lays down the critical rule for all our God-talk: *"God is always ever greater."* Greater than our affirmations. Greater than our negations. Greater than what we can say or think. Greater than what we can understand or even desire to understand.

As we strive to find the least misguided and misleading ways of thinking about God, we are making ourselves available for transformation, a transformation that takes us out into the mystery that lies beyond anything we could imagine, much less put into words. In his Gifford lectures, Rowan Williams argued that we have to submit our language about God to the truth that the divine reality is endlessly excessive: it cannot be spoken of or thought about finally or exhaustively. God is infinitely self-determined and absolutely unconditioned and uncontrolled. In coming to that realization, we show that God is not a reality we are making for ourselves, not a projection of our own thoughts. Just for that reason, we have to speak about God carefully, discerningly, humbly. Coming to know God truly is inseparably bound with the practice of *unknowing*, with what Nicholas of Cusa styled "learned ignorance" and Sarah Coakley has called unmastery. Our thinking and speaking about God cannot explain the divine mystery, but it can, by grace, identify God faithfully. As Maximus Confessor put it, genuine faith makes possible the supreme ignorance that is required to know the supremely unknowable one. Perhaps this is why Jesus so sharply challenged the wealthy young synagogue ruler who asked what good work had to been done to find eternal life. "Why do you ask me about what is good? There is only one who is good." By forcing the man to question himself and his thinking, Jesus creates space for his conversion and ultimate transformation. If the man lets Christ put all his convictions to the test, he can be delivered from his illusions. If he desires truly to know why it is that he has called Jesus good, he will make himself available for the transforming vision of the God Jesus reveals.

***

We see the way of transformational negation opened up for us in Balaam's song to Balaak (described in Numbers) and St. Paul's sermon to the Athenians (described in Acts). Prophet and apostle alike identify who God is by affirming what he is not. Balaam: "God is not a human being, that he should lie, or a mortal, that he should change his mind. Has he promised, and will he not do it?" Paul: "God who made the world and everything in it . . . does not live in shrines made by human hands, nor is he served by human hands, as though he needed anything, since he himself gives to all mortals life and breath and all things."

Attending to their wisdom, we learn, first, that God is not an existent in the universe, not one of the things that exists. In fact, to put it even more pointedly, we can say with Aquinas that God does not exist at all: God simply is his own existence. If that just seems wrong, think about it like this. Imagine a chalkboard. On that board, draw a circle and then fill it with X's of various sizes and colors. Let those marks represent everything that exists, from archangels to amoeba, from love to licorice. We are tempted to think of God as the largest X in the circle, or perhaps as the circle itself. But God is neither the circle nor one of the marks within it. God is, instead, more like the chalk and chalkboard and the event of marking. He is whatever it is that makes the circle a circle and the X's the distinct marks that they are. In the language of Scripture, the triune God is "before all things, and in him all things hold together." That there's anything at all, rather than nothing, is due to the fact that God "upholds all things by the word of his power." Understanding this, we can see what Simone Weil means when she says that it is purifying to pray to God not only in secret as far as our neighbors are concerned, but also with the thought "that God does not exist." By putting to death our imaginations of God as an existent, withdrawing into the dark night of divine hiddenness, God saves us from loving him as the "miser loves his gold." In this way, the cancer of idolatry is cut away from the organ of genuine faith—a surgery that has to take place again and again and again over the course of our lives.

***

We learn, second, that God is not sometimes present and active, sometimes absent and passive. God is not an (awesomely powerful, incredibly knowledgeable) agent among other (less powerful, less knowledgeable) agents. When we say that God is omnipotent, we don't mean that God has the most power in the universe, power enough to overcome any and all resistances to his will. No, we mean that God has all the divine power there is. Only God is God. Everything else is not God. And that means that no creature has any (divine) power whatsoever; it has only the (creaturely) power given to it by its creator. As Jesus reminded Pilate, "You would have no power over me unless it had been given you from above" (John 19:11). In the same way, when we say that God is omnipresent, we don't mean that God is capable of being anywhere he wants to be whenever he wants to be. We mean that God, as his own presence, is always present to us. God is an event, a happening, "not an object but a Life that is going on eternally and yet ever new," as Hans Urs von Balthasar put it. In the words of Aquinas, God is "pure act"—and as such always fully all that he is. What does that mean? It means that if he weren't actively present, holding us in being, ever nearer to us than we are to ourselves, we wouldn't be ourselves at all.

We don't experience God in this way, obviously. But a little reflection finds that that is just what we should expect. God's presence must be revealed to us—as we trust it will be in the End. For now, however, we know that presence only by faith, and our lives remain hidden in God even as God's presence remains hidden from us. Perhaps no one understood this better than St. John of the Cross: no sensible experience is proof of God's presence any more than the lack of sensible experience is proof of God's absence. Because God always works with what St John calls "the condition of our mortal life," we know that any "impression" that comes to us is not to be confused with the gracious presence of God that upholds us. No feelings, however profound, ever bring us nearer to God or God to us. In the same way, no lack of feelings can take us away from God. When all impressions fail, leaving us in "dryness, darkness, and desolation," we should not even for a moment think that God is far from us. Nothing can separate us from the love that holds us in being, least of all our feelings. This is why St John of the Cross says that God is nearest to us when we are least aware of it.

***

Third, and finally, we learn that God is not in any way constrained or obligated. In the course of talking about what we believe, we often suggest or imply that God is subject to eternity as we are subject to time/space. As if God lives in and is conditioned by living in heaven like we are by living on earth. We also often suggest that in his dealings with us God remains subject to the rules of justice or to moral principles imagined as external to and other than God himself. But this simply cannot be true. Utterly unlike all created things, God is uniquely, absolutely free—free from all rivals, free from all laws. God is conditioned by nothing but God: this is the critical truth of the doctrine of *creatio ex nihilo*. It may at first seem merely academic, but reflection reveals it is at the heart of our faith. Saying that God creates from nothing means that everything that exists is other than God, and utterly dependent on God. And it also means that God has no needs and so cannot be manipulated or used.

A needy God would be the worst possible reality, because it would mean both our existence and our salvation are ulteriorly motivated. A needy God can give no gifts; he can only strike bargains or offer rewards. And precisely for that reason a needy God is inherently vulnerable to manipulation. Once we know what such a God needs, we can use it against him, drawing him into service of our purposes just as we do with all other idols. Such a God would not and could not decide to be God *for us,* assuming our humanity as his own. Such a God would not and could not submit to the humiliations of torture and death to deliver us from the powers of alienation estranging us from ourselves and our world. Such a God would not and could not make room for us within his own life, sharing all that he has with us.

The good news is that God is *not* needy. God is conditioned by nothing, and so is in no way vulnerable to manipulation. And just for that reason we can trust the divine promises, and can rest in the hope that the end purposed for us is good as he is good. God does not need our love, or our worship, or our obedience. God does not create or redeem us to meet some lack in his life. He creates and saves for nothing but *our* good. All that he does, like all that he is, is gift. To see that is to live in the light.

CHAPTER THREE

Saving Desire

"One thing I have desired of the Lord . . .
to behold the beauty of the Lord, and to inquire in his temple."

Psalm 27:4

"He had no form or beauty that we should look to him,
nothing in his appearance that we should desire him."

Isaiah 53:2

Why do we love God? When we find ourselves desiring God, what is it that we find desirable and lovely? How is it that we come to love this particular God in the first place? And what is the source of this loving? What is its goal? Scripture reveals that we love God because God first loved us. But we should not take this to mean our love for God is a self-determined response. We love God because we are graced to do so. Or, to say the same thing another way, we love God because God loves our love for God into being. All that God requires of us God first makes possible for us, and then leads us into that possibility—and just so into our fulfillment.

What we love about God is rightly called his beauty. But at least for those of us who believe that the truth about God is

revealed in the story of a particularly scandalous Palestinian peas-
ant, what a strange beauty it turns out to be. Perhaps we shouldn't
be so surprised by that strangeness, after all. It is *God's* beauty, and
precisely for that reason a loveliness we cannot fashion on our own
and would not even if we could. This divine beauty is not only unimaginable for us, it is unbecoming by our standards, and we have
to suffer it patiently if we ever hope to see it for what it truly is. As
St. Paul reminds us, God's wisdom seems like so much foolishness to our common sense and his power appears weak compared
with our illusions of mastery (1 Cor 1:18–31). To be sure, we are
creatures made for God, and so in some sense naturally desire
him. He is, as Augustine said, our homeland. But what if we are
so afraid, so caught up in untruth, so weary with our own failures,
so bewildered by the wrongs done to us, that we do not find him
desirable? Or, to say the same thing more traditionally, what if we
are so diseased by sin that we can't bring ourselves to love God as
God is and love our neighbor as ourselves?

Before moving on, I do want to say this as clearly as I can:
when in worship we confess that we are sinners, we are not engaging in self-hatred or self-abuse. Just the opposite, in fact. We are
acknowledging to ourselves and to others before God our absolute
helplessness to live the lives we want and need to live. We are acknowledging that we can only receive what we need as God freely
graces us to receive it. We are acknowledging that we can only see
God's beauty as God opens our eyes to it.

That may, at first, sound like bad news. But in fact this is the
ground of all our hope: God is not our creation but our creator,
not what we make him out to be, but what he in fact is by virtue
of his own life wholly apart from us. And just because he is lovely
in himself he can make us lovely, awakening us to the truth of his
beauty so that we both see him as he is and become like him in that
seeing. I said in the previous chapter that nothing is more fitting
or freeing for us than contemplating God's beauty. The good news
is that God makes that reality possible by sharing his own life, his
own loveliness, with us. What is uniquely his, he makes ours.

***

But we are too easily deceived by our desires—especially by our desires for the transcendence and eternity that determine the ultimate meaning of our lives. The Gospels teach us that many of those who crowded around Jesus, including some of his closest disciples and dearest friends, were drawn to him by false hopes and vain expectations. The hard truth is that we too often find ourselves attracted to what we wrongly think is God. At times, like Simon the Sorcerer, we come seeking God for those powers we find useful, imagining that by professing belief in God we have secured a resource that will afford us the life we want for ourselves (Acts 8:9–25). But for most of us, at least most of the time, the deception is more subtle, less complete. Our desires are not so much out-and-out corrupt as ever-so-slightly bent. We delight in the justice of God, but at least in part because we imagine it means grief for our enemies. We delight in the mercy of God, but at least in part because we imagine it frees us from responsibility to work for justice in the world. We delight in the power of God, but at least in part because we imagine it means we are protected from sufferings others have to face. We delight in the truth of God, but at least in part because we take pride in being right, and we want to be known as knowledgeable and wise. We delight in the law of God, but at least in part because we imagine it provides a moral framework that allows us to sort neatly right from wrong, order from disorder, the good folks from the bad folks. We delight in the calling of God, but at least in part because we imagine it means we can find success in ministry and make a name for ourselves. We delight in the presence and work of God in our lives, but at least in part because we like how that experience leaves us feeling and we want to advance quickly into the depths and heights of our faith.

We are always, until the end, living at the risk of these deceptions and countless others like them. But we do not need to panic or to despair. If we desire what is good in ways that are not good, we can rest assured that God will gracefully disappoint us. If what we find delightful in God is in fact an illusion, God has promised to go on revealing his true beauty until we find that beauty truly desirable.

***

But how does God do this? If we find God-as-he-is undesirable, if we are attracted to what is merely a projection of immature or confused desires, if we have launched ourselves with all good intentions toward a goal that is not in fact attainable, then how can we receive the good we need to be truly ourselves? Answering that question brings us to the heart of the gospel: we can find God beautiful only as he both makes himself fully present and available to us and creates in us the power to respond in kind. Only God can know God, and only God can lead us into knowing as we are known. We cannot save ourselves from ourselves, and the most precious gifts are those we cannot but receive. We are creatures, and so radically, utterly dependent on God for our salvation no less than for our existence. In fact, if the gospel is true, we are free to be saved only because we are the creatures that we are: finite, temporal, embodied. And God is free to save us just because he is the God he is: infinite, triune, and incarnate. Because God is three-as-one, and has taken our humanity as his own, he can make us beautiful with his own beauty without in any sense violating our creaturely integrity or unmaking our particularities as human persons.

In taking our humanity as his own, however, God scandalizes and offends us. As Bonhoeffer reminds us in his christology lectures, the incarnation is not a humiliation for *God*—it is not as if God finds it unbecoming to take humanity as his own! The incarnation is a humiliation for *us*, because God comes among us as one without beauty, without desirability or comeliness, making nonsense of every frame of reference, every standard of judgment, every order and scheme we have devised for ourselves as a means of giving our lives significance and stability. Simone Weil has it right, I think: "through the operation of the dark night, God withdraws himself in order not to be loved like the treasure is by the miser."

What offends us, therefore, is the revelation that God is humble, and that it is only as we humble ourselves—counting as nothing all of the achievements and privileges that assure us of our significance and refusing all of the structures that secure us against the threats of our enemies—that we can truly be ourselves, at home in the world we've been given, ready to bear responsibilities for our neighbors. God loves us too much to let us settle for the god of our own imagining. He scandalizes us in order to deliver us from illusion.

***

Why do we exist? Why does anything at all exist? According to the Scriptures, "all things were created through Christ and for him," and in the end he, with us—co-laborers in his humiliation and co-inheritors in his exaltation—will return creation to the Father so that God may be "all in all." This truth is basic to everything else we believe: creation comes about not through any need or lack in the divine life. Creation comes about just because God's life is an endless, always-excessive exchange of the gift of the divine nature. At every point, therefore, creation remains dependent on the infinite generosity and hospitality of God. And our joy, our fulfillment, comes in participation in that eternally generous and hospitable event.

With that understanding, we recognize sin as whatever it is that frustrates or defaces our joy, whatever it is that keeps us from resting in the event of God that is the source of our life. Tragically, the power of sin is such that it can and does keep us from that joy, that rest—and just so from being ourselves. If, then, we are to know the life purposed for us, we must be redeemed, delivered, reconciled, healed. How does God do this? In the same way that he exists and creates: by *love*, triunely given and received.

That said, it is important to notice that redemption differs from creation in at least one respect: God must take up *both* the giving *and* the receiving for us. He cannot simply give himself to us, because sin keeps us from receiving his gift as gift. So he must receive his own gift for us, and do it in such a way that we have generated within us the capacity to enjoy the life we're purposed to live. For us to be ourselves, God must destroy the power of sin that enslaves us, setting us free to be loved and to love, delivering us to share in the joy unspeakable that the divine life eternally is.

With creation, God suffers no pain, no loss. With redemption, however, he does. Notice how often the New Testament speaks in terms like these: the Father must give up his Son and the Son must both give himself over for us to death and give himself into the Father's hands in obedience unto death. In order to destroy sin, the divine life has in the humanity of the Son taken into itself the horrors of sin and death—the thanklessness, the ignorance, the pretension, the fear. Gloriously, however, God's love is too much for death as light is too much for darkness and laughter too much for weeping. The giving and receiving of the Father, Son, and Spirit triumph in the flesh of Christ over all the powers that would un-make us and our world.

***

Although the triune God is always holding us up, our redemption isn't complete, isn't truly ours, until we find ourselves loving as God loves. God's work in us won't be consummated until we can love one another, ourselves, and every created thing with the same love that the triune God is and makes possible. That and nothing less than that is what God desires for us and effects in us.

But so many of our desires are chronically, even fatally, diseased. At times, we find ourselves hyper-aware of what's happening, eaten up with unholy dissatisfactions, complaining about what we don't have or grumbling about what we do. Other times, we are almost entirely unaware of what's happening, hardly sensitive at all to the beauty bursting forth around us, shining in the face of this neighbor, that stranger.

So what is our hope? How can we be healed? God saves us from bad desires (what St. Augustine calls disordered loves) by taking us up into God's own desire—for God and for us. In the incarnation, God humanizes the divine desire and divinizes human desires. Because that work is accomplished, the Spirit now is drawing us into communion with Jesus, the one who embodies human desire wholly aligned with the divine desire, and so reorders our loves. We might even say that the life of the Spirit is nothing other than the movement of the Son's desire for the Father and the Father's delight in the Son. And it is that life, that movement, that has taken us up for our good.

Talking about the Spirit in such terms reminds us that when we tell the story of Jesus's life and death, we should not talk as if the Father and the Son are the only ones acting. In a sense, it is the Spirit who makes all of their work possible. The Spirit is the freedom through which the Father' gives and gives up the Son, and through which the Father receives the Son again. The Spirit is the power by which the Son gives himself over to death and offers himself up to the Father in such a way that the Father's inexhaustible love for the world is made known. The Spirit is the wisdom that makes the Father's love for us and for his only begotten Son, as well as the Son's love for his Father and for us, always indivisibly one and the same love. The Spirit is the grace that holds the Father and the divine-human Son in their mutually determining intimacy—even on the cross, even in death. Because the Spirit bridges the empty distance of sin and death, we do not exist outside of the reach of the divine love: this is why nothing can separate us from the love of God in Christ Jesus. Because the Spirit is the Spirit, nothing that exists exists outside or apart from the presence of the love that God triunely is. "Even in hell, you are there."

This truth comes into stark relief in the juxtaposition of two Pauline texts: First, Romans 8:15–17, 26–27:

> For you did not receive a spirit of slavery to fall back into fear, but you have received a spirit of adoption. When we cry, "Abba! Father!" it is that very Spirit bearing witness with our spirit that we are children of God, and if

children, then heirs, heirs of God and joint heirs with
Christ—if, in fact, we suffer with him so that we may also
be glorified with him. . . . Likewise the Spirit helps us in
our weakness; for we do not know how to pray as we
ought, but that very Spirit intercedes with sighs too deep
for words. And God, who searches the heart, knows what
is the mind of the Spirit, because the Spirit intercedes for
the saints according to the will of God.

And then, 1 Corinthians 2:10, 13–16:

These things God has revealed to us through the Spirit;
for the Spirit searches everything, even the depths of
God. And we speak of these things in words not taught
by human wisdom but taught by the Spirit, interpreting
spiritual things to those who are spiritual. Those who
are unspiritual do not receive the gifts of God's Spirit,
for they are foolishness to them, and they are unable to
understand them because they are spiritually discerned.
Those who are spiritual discern all things, and they are
themselves subject to no one else's scrutiny. "For who has
known the mind of the Lord so as to instruct him?" But
we have the mind of Christ.

Reading these texts closely, we see that the Spirit searches the
depths of the Father, and discovers there for us the mind, the character, of Christ. And we see that the Father searches our hearts,
coming to know us in and through the Spirit's intimacy with us as
giver and sustainer of our life. The Father searches us as the Spirit
searches the Father, and what the Father finds in us is the need for
the fullness of divine life which the Spirit discovers for us in the
Father's depths. The Spirit knows God as God is and knows us as
we are, and in that knowing draws us into God's own communion
with God so that we are at-one-ed with him, joined to him as bone
of Christ's bone and flesh of his flesh.

God is lovely because God is lover, loved, and love itself, giving and receiving love in a way perfectly fitting for his own infinite life. Richard of St. Victor makes the argument something like this: God is love because the Father loves the Son with the love only God can give, and the Son receives and reciprocates this love in the way only God can receive and reciprocate it. In the same way, the Father and the Son together co-love the Spirit, who, in receiving this perfectly shared love, is freed to love the Father and the Son into loving one another beyond selfishness. And because this is the God in whose image we are made, it is only as we come to gaze on this beauty that we begin to become our true selves, bodying forth the fearless love from which and for which we are made.

A few years ago, I had all of this brought to bear on me unexpectedly and unforgettably. My in-laws had come in from Oklahoma, and my mother-in-law had brought gifts for my kids. Zoë, my oldest, had a gift ready to give back to her. My middle son, Clive, seeing this, left the gift he had just received and ran upstairs to his room, and came back, moments later, with a book—which, believe it or not, my mother-in-law had given to him some other time. I could see that he was torn: he so desperately wanted to give her a gift in return, but he also loved this book that she had given him and he didn't want to be without it. She saw his hesitation too, and quickly knelt down, put her arm around him, and reassured him: "Thank you for this gift, Clive! I don't want you to be without it when I'm back at home. Can we keep it here at your house so that whenever I'm here with you, we can read it together?"

Surely *that* is the kind of change God means to work in us. To be drawn into God's beauty is to have our lives so taken up in the moment of gift that we lose all sense of where the giving ends and the receiving begins. Becoming one with the Three whose life is perfect delight, we're translated into a whole new realm of being, becoming, in ways we would never have even dared to imagine, truly ourselves.

CHAPTER FOUR

Practicing the Absence of God

"You are a God who hides himself, God of Israel, Savior."
Isaiah 45:15

"I said to my soul, be still, and let the dark come upon you,
which shall be the darkness of God."

T. S. Eliot

We talk—too much, arguably—about the presence of God. At least, we often talk too glibly about it. We talk as if that presence comes and goes depending on how intensely we desire it. We talk as if our desires for God's presence are always a good and pure. We talk as if God's presence is something simply to be enjoyed. But all of these assumptions, betrayed in myriad ways in our speech and in our actions, need to be challenged.

First, God's presence does not come and go. Certainly not in response to our desire for it. God is nearer to us than we are to ourselves, closer than our own consciousness, nearer than our very being. In the words as Nicholas Cabasilas, God is "more a part of us than our own limbs, more necessary to us than our own heart." All of us can sing, as St Augustine did, in the realization that

God is with and within us even though we are without him. We are the ones who come and go from the presence.

Of course, at times we find ourselves desiring God, seeking God. But in truth we only seek God because we are already found. The deepest truth is not that we know God, but that we are known by him. And God's knowing of us is always already previous to our knowing of God. Even our searching is a gift. As Aslan says to Jill in C. S. Lewis' *The Silver Chair*: "You would not have called to me if I had not been calling to you."

***

Second, our desires for God are not always pure. In fact, they never are, even at their best. They must always be redeemed, purified, set right, reconstituted, healed. Eliot (in "East Coker") gets this right, I believe:

> I said to my soul, be still, and wait without hope
> > For hope would be hope for the wrong thing; wait
> without love
> > For love would be love of the wrong thing; there is
> yet faith
> > But the faith and the love and the hope are all in the
> waiting.
> > Wait without thought, for you are not ready for
> thought:
> > So the darkness shall be the light, and the stillness
> the dancing.

He can wait in this fashion only because he has already accepted that the darkness that is coming is "the darkness of God," a darkness that is like the dimming of the lights in the theatre so the scene can be changed. Surely, that is why God lets the darkness come, leads us into "dark night." Only there can God effect the changes necessary to move us from the false to the true, from selfishness to charity.

And we can trust that God will over time effect the necessary changes. The physician will heal us. The teacher will train us. But

we must be ready for the trouble of that healing and training. As
Rowan Williams warns, "If you genuinely desire union with the
unspeakable love of God, then you must be prepared to have your
'religious' world shattered." God will be against us for our sake.
God is our friend, and, as Scripture promises, "faithful are the
wounds of a friend."

How does God shatter these illusions? By showing us, again
and again, the image of Christ the crucified one. By showing us the
beauty of the one who is undesirable by all our standards. As we
"with unveiled faces" behold *that* image—in the face of the stranger, in the face of the enemy, in the face of the neighbor—we begin
slowly to be transformed from glory to glory into its likeness.

***

Third, God's presence is not something simply to be enjoyed. God's
presence is glorious—heavy, burdensome. "The hand of the Lord
was heavy upon me," the prophets say. If, like David, we pray for
God not to take his Holy Spirit from us (Ps 51:11), it is not because
we always enjoy what the Spirit brings to us. So much of what he
gives us to drink has a bitter taste. How could we possibly enjoy
loving our enemies, turning the other cheek to those who abuse us,
going the extra mile for those who take advantage us?

J. H. King, an early Pentecostal missionary and churchman,
drew on the story of Ishmael and Isaac to show how God requires
us to give up not only what should never have been in our lives at
all but also that which is in our lives only because of God's goodness. Our experience of God must be crucified, King says, because
we will find the "ecstasies of joy," the "peace of heaven" so sweet we
begin to feel that the experience is essential to our living faithfully.
But "we shall come to the point where God will lead us away from
these ecstasies . . . and as a result we shall sink deeper into him."

As King recognizes, many of us too often want simply to
forget our responsibilities to our neighbors and throw ourselves
down in the sweetness of the experience of God. Meister Eckert,
the medieval German theologian, recognized this dynamic in

Mary's devotion to Jesus and Martha's complaints about her sister in Luke 10:38–42.

> Martha was afraid her sister would remain clinging to consolation and sweetness, and she wished her to become as she herself was. This is why Christ said, "She has chosen the best part," as if to say, "Cheer up, Martha; this will leave her. The most sublime thing that can happen to a creature shall happen to her: She shall become as happy as you."

Mary did learn as she listened to the Lord's teaching. But *what* she learned was the calling to live prayerfully in the world, amidst the goings-on of day-to-day life. And this, Eckhart says, is how the saints become saints: they learn to serve their neighbors prayerfully, rather than turning from their neighbors to prayer and the experience of God.

Mary, like "Doubting" Thomas, needed to learn how to practice the absence of God. She had to come to understand, as he did, that it is more blessed not to see. She had to recognize that the "presence" she had known was nothing compared to the "absence" she was about to experience, an absence created so she would not only be *with* Christ but *in* him. Before this moment, Jesus was simply another body in the room for her, one more person in her life. After this moment, Mary recognized Jesus as the room itself, the Father's house, and the very source of her life. And we, like St Thomas, like Mary, and like her sister, Martha, must come to know that we are called not to enjoy the presence but to be that presence for others.

***

Job complains that no matter where he turns, God remains hidden from him: "If I go forward, he is not there; or backward, I cannot perceive him; on the left he hides, and I cannot behold him; I turn to the right, but I cannot see him" (Job 23:8–9). But Paul reveals why it is that God is neither here nor there for us: "I pray that you may have the power to comprehend, with all the saints, what is the breadth and length and height and depth, and to know the love of Christ that surpasses knowledge, so that you may be filled with all the fullness of God" (Eph 3:19–20). The truth is, we cannot locate God as an object of perception because we are held in the infinite dimensions of his love for us. And not only held—we are opened up to receive that very fullness so that we become the site of God's presence as it is happening in the world. God may be hidden from us, but that is only because God is so near to our neighbor that who he is and who we are have become inseparably bound up together. As Bonhoeffer says, "The Christian person achieves his true nature when God no longer confronts him as Thou but 'enters in' to him as I." The absence of God is nothing but God being present in and through us to those most in need.

CHAPTER FIVE

Blessed Are Those Who Do Not See

"The devil dazzles; Christ does not."

MIROSLAV VOLF

"Blessed are those who have not seen and yet believe."

JOHN 20:29

Everything comes down to how we perceive and interpret the world. Everything depends on our seeing—and our not-seeing. Tragically, we have not as a rule developed the knowledge, skills, and character necessary for faithful discernment and sound judgment. We have not been trained to see and not-see as Christ himself does. What is more, we have been stupified by the cares of this life, by the attacks of the enemy, and by pride in our own moral and religious efforts so that we are increasingly desensitized to the reality of the Holy Spirit and hyper-sensitized to the realities of the spirit of the age. As a result, we are ever at risk of leaning on our own understanding while assuming that we are trusting in the Lord.

St. John weaves themes of seeing/not seeing from beginning to end of his Gospel. He bookends the stories of Moses and Thomas, insisting, first, that no one has ever seen God—not even Moses, who according to the Scripture beheld God's glory (1:17–18)—and then concluding that it is truly more blessed not to see and still to believe (20:29).

Arguably, the story of the man born blind in John 9 brings the Johannine understanding of vision/blindness most forcefully to bear. The story emphasizes the characters' frames of interpretation, the hidden convictions that predetermine what they can and cannot see in one another and in Christ. We might take this story, then, as paradigmatic, allowing it to put our own moral vision, our capacity for discerning the truth, to the test.

> As he walked along, he saw a man blind from birth. His disciples asked him, "Rabbi, who sinned, this man or his parents, that he was born blind?" Jesus answered, "Neither this man nor his parents sinned; he was born blind so that God's works might be revealed in him. We must work the works of him who sent me while it is day; night is coming when no one can work. As long as I am in the world, I am the light of the world." When he had said this, he spat on the ground and made mud with the saliva and spread the mud on the man's eyes, saying to him, "Go, wash in the pool of Siloam" (which means Sent). Then he went and washed and came back able to see. The neighbors and those who had seen him before as a beggar began to ask, "Is this not the man who used to sit and beg?" Some were saying, "It is he." Others were saying, "No, but it is someone like him." He kept saying, "I am the man." But they kept asking him, "Then how were your eyes opened?" He answered, "The man called Jesus made mud, spread it on my eyes, and said to me, 'Go to Siloam and wash.' Then I went and washed and received my sight." They said to him, "Where is he?" He said, "I do not know." They brought to the Pharisees the man who had formerly been blind. Now it was a sabbath day when Jesus made the mud and opened his eyes. Then the Pharisees also began to ask him how he had received

his sight. He said to them, "He put mud on my eyes. Then I washed, and now I see." Some of the Pharisees said, "This man is not from God, for he does not observe the sabbath." But others said, "How can a man who is a sinner perform such signs?" And they were divided. So they said again to the blind man, "What do you say about him? It was your eyes he opened." He said, "He is a prophet."

Jesus's miracle, stunning and spectacular as it is, convinces exactly no one of his messiahship. Indeed, it could not convince anyone because it was not seen in the light of faith. On this score, the disciples turn out to be no less blind than the Pharisees are. The former cannot see Jesus in his glory because they assume this man has sinned and has been blinded by God as a punishment for his sins. The latter cannot see Jesus in his glory because they suspect that he healed the man through some devious power. Even the man himself, after being healed, remains unaware of who Jesus is and what exactly has happened to him. He knows no more than the crowds who are dumbstruck by what has happened. Tellingly, he makes no confession of faith. He simply states the facts as he experienced them: "I was blind, and now I see." When he's forced finally to give an opinion, he says only that Jesus must be a prophet.

> The Jews did not believe that he had been blind and had received his sight until they called the parents of the man who had received his sight and asked them, "Is this your son, who you say was born blind? How then does he now see?" His parents answered, "We know that this is our son, and that he was born blind; but we do not know how it is that now he sees, nor do we know who opened his eyes. Ask him; he is of age. He will speak for himself." His parents said this because they were afraid of the Jews; for the Jews had already agreed that anyone who confessed Jesus to be the Messiah would be put out of the synagogue. Therefore his parents said, "He is of age; ask him." So for the second time they called the man who had been blind, and they said to him, "Give glory to God! We know that this man is a sinner." He answered, "I do not know whether he is a sinner. One

thing I do know, that though I was blind, now I see." They said to him, "What did he do to you? How did he open your eyes?" He answered them, "I have told you already, and you would not listen. Why do you want to hear it again? Do you also want to become his disciples?" Then they reviled him, saying, "You are his disciple, but we are disciples of Moses. We know that God has spoken to Moses, but as for this man, we do not know where he comes from." The man answered, "Here is an astonishing thing! You do not know where he comes from, and yet he opened my eyes. We know that God does not listen to sinners, but he does listen to one who worships him and obeys his will. Never since the world began has it been heard that anyone opened the eyes of a person born blind. If this man were not from God, he could do nothing." They answered him, "You were born entirely in sins, and are you trying to teach us?" And they drove him out. Jesus heard that they had driven him out, and when he found him, he said, "Do you believe in the Son of Man?" He answered, "And who is he, sir? Tell me, so that I may believe in him." Jesus said to him, "You have seen him, and the one speaking with you is he." He said, "Lord, I believe." And he worshiped him. Jesus said, "I came into this world for judgment so that those who do not see may see, and those who do see may become blind." Some of the Pharisees near him heard this and said to him, "Surely we are not blind, are we?" Jesus said to them, "If you were blind, you would not have sin. But now that you say, 'We see,' your sin remains."

***

What do we learn from his story? We learn that Christ opens the eyes of the blind, and that he does so simply because he desires good for us and not in response to our faith or faithfulness. We learn that his ways of healing us are often strange, even bizarre, at least compared to what we've known as normal. We learn that our blindness is not the result of our failures, but the result of a condition into which we are thrown from birth; we are not only sinners but also—and even more deeply, more primally—sinned against. We learn that we can and should be as disarmingly honest as this blind man, owning without pretense what we in fact do not know or cannot comprehend, never claiming to believe more than we in fact do. After all, what makes our witness faithful is not our expertise or our certainty, but the constant acknowledgment of our (at best) imperfect understanding of what the Lord is doing and the constant trust that we are known and loved even as we are ignorant and unfaithful. As St Paul puts it, "Anyone who claims to know something does not yet have the necessary knowledge; but anyone who loves God is known by him" (1 Cor 8:2). Finally, we learn not only that we must have our eyes opened so that we can see the glory of God, but also that we must be blinded to the vainglorious illusions of the world. The vision Christ gives is *both* enlightening *and* blinding.

An old altar song promises that if we turn our eyes upon Jesus the "things of this earth/will grow strangely dim/in the light of his glory and grace." At first blush, the message seems to be all wrong. Surely, we might say—as I in fact have often said—it is in the light of Christ's glory that our eyes are *opened* to reality, not closed to it. As Scripture declares, in his light we see light. Only in Christ are we enabled to see God and neighbor as they truly are. And yet, there is a truth in the song's message. The glory of God in the face of Jesus Christ *does* blind us—to the unrealities of the world, to the lies we have been told and tell ourselves, to the fantasies that our enemy uses to our destruction. In Christ, we are closed to racist stereotypes and to the obtuse standards of attractiveness that oppress our sisters and our mothers, our wives and our daughters. In Christ, we find we are turned toward the fullness of God and neighbor, and turned away from the emptiness of worldly power and selfish ambition. Enlightened by his love, we refuse to regard the borders drawn by political powers as finally authoritative in our care for refugees and immigrants. And in times of war, we refuse to allow patriotic sentimentality to sanction hatred for a supposed enemy.

Rowan Williams argues that what makes the saints saintly is their openness to judgment, their "readiness to be questioned, judged, stripped naked, and left speechless by that which lies at the center of their faith." To be holy, in other words, is to live blinded by the truth. And this is because they share in Jesus's love-blindness. In the language of Isaiah (42:18–20):

> Listen, you that are deaf;
> and you that are blind, look up and see!
> Who is blind but my servant,
> or deaf like my messenger whom I send?
> Who is blind like my dedicated one,
> or blind like the servant of the LORD?
> He sees many things, but does not observe them;
> his ears are open, but he does not hear.

The Gospels make it clear: Jesus saw people in the fullness of their humanity. He did not see "the poor"; he saw a particular poor man; he did not see "widows and orphans"; he saw this particular widow, that particular orphan. In the same way, we can love one another with Christ's love only if we are also blind to the "issues" that are used to define people. We must not see "the sick" or "the oppressed" or "the marginalized" but specific people suffering in particular ways. We must come alongside them and be to them the providence of God. We must look at them and see what God says is true about them—nothing more, and nothing less. After all, this is how we ourselves are known. And remembering this, we recognize what it means to be blessed because we do not see.

CHAPTER SIX

God Is Not in Control

"I am God, and . . . there is no one who can deliver from my hand;
I work and who can hinder it?"

ISAIAH 43:13

"I am the LORD, and there is no other;
besides me there is no god."

ISAIAH 45:5

L et me begin by defending the devil. Strange as such a move may seem, it is easy to underestimate how masterfully devious he in fact is. Only Jesus's victory over him can expose his tricks for what they are. And what we find when we read the story of the wilderness temptations closely is that Satan is not so much tempting us to disbelieve as to believe unfaithfully. Again and again, he entices Jesus to use God's word against him, to claim God's truth in a false way. And the same holds for our temptations: Satan wants us to take God's promises to mean what they do not in fact mean, so that we are confused about what we can and should expect from God.

Perhaps that is where we too often find ourselves: believing strongly—but in misunderstandings of God's word. We trust God as provider, but rely on our own sense of need. We trust God as healer, but assume we know what health is. We trust God as deliverer and protector, but expect that deliverance to come on our own terms and in our own time. In these and in countless other ways we are so much of the time taxed by false expectations and bad desires, waiting on God to do what God is not going to do—at least not in the way that we expect it to be done. And so we move from suffering to suffering, from frustration to frustration, from disappointment to disappointment, not because God is unfaithful, but because our expectations of God are stubbornly perverse. We have turned the bread of God's promises into stones of distrust.

What are we to do, then? How do we right our expectations? We must contemplate the living God as he has made himself known to us in Christ. And we must give time for that contemplation to convert our imaginations, to free us from the illusions that blind us and from the passions that enslave us.

In many ways, our move toward a mature grasp of the truth begins in the recognition that God is not in control of what happens in the world, and that all that we experience in this world is at best an incomplete realization of God's will for us. Perhaps we want to think God is in control because of our own fantasies for control or our own anxieties of being controlled. Regardless, we have to come to terms with the fact that God is not in control— even as we confess in faith that God is sovereign.

***

Saying God is sovereign means that God is not at the mercy of what happens in the world, does not suffer change as all creatures must, and is not in any rivalry with, much less under the control of, some other power. God is not and cannot be caught off guard or surprised. God is God and everything that exists does so only in radical dependence on his sovereignty.

But sovereignty is utterly other than what we have known as control. Control makes something act in ways false to itself. It violates, overpowers, coerces, masters. Control takes away freedom, forcing someone or something to do what is against its own nature or will. And God, as creator, simply does not—and indeed, cannot—do that kind of violence. God gives being to creatures, affording them their freedom, their integrity. To say that God is sovereign is to say that God does not need control to get his will done. He does not have to destroy our freedom to express his own; he does not have to subjugate us to make himself known as Lord. God's sovereignty is such that his freedom is not at odds with our freedom, and his Lordship does not subjugate but frees and empowers and fulfills. Creatures overpower; God reigns. And that reign is absolutely identical with God's love.

I recently heard a sermon in which the preacher argued that God, like the engineers at Disney World who work from a control center underground, is "at the controls," monitoring what is happening with us, assuring that we have the best time possible. But nothing could be further from the truth. God is not standing at some remove, observing what is happening with us, acting in ways that secure us against trouble or difficulty. God is not a mind that observes but a spirit that acts and interacts. But that interaction happens over time (and upon time) in ways we cannot imagine or anticipate.

Luther said that if all we had to go on was our experience of the world, we would have to conclude either that God does not exist or that God is evil. But by faith we see more than our experience of the world: we see God, and hear his promises to set all wrongs right. Until the end, therefore, when God's will is finally fully done, we have to maintain a distinction between what happens and what God is doing, trusting that nothing happens apart from God's will but that not everything that happens is itself God's will. Or to say the same thing another way, everything that happens takes place *within* the will of God but not everything that happens *is* the will of

God. What is more, nothing that happens is God's will in fullness. Whatever happens, then, and whatever God does, we are left waiting for the fullness of God's action, and so we pray, even after God has acted, "Let your will be done on earth as it is in heaven" (Matt 6:10). We will keep praying this prayer until the end of all things, which finally God will answer that prayer.

In 1993, while on assignment in Sudan, journalist Kevin Carter took a photograph of a young girl, nearly dead from starvation, with a vulture hulking nearby, waiting for its prey to die.

What are we to say about this moment? How is it related to the will of God? And what of all the other moments of tragedy, injustice, and evil that take place in the world? Why doesn't God intervene to save this little girl? Or the thousands of other children who starved to death during the famine? If God can stop it from happening, then why doesn't he? If God cannot stop it, then what do we mean when we talk about God being sovereign? We need not say that God "had a plan" in which the death of this child played some necessary part. And we don't need to say that God could not do anything about it, not even because of chosen self-limitations: God does not have to be less than God for creatures to be all that they are. It is best, I think, to say that this death took place not *as* the will of God, but within the unfolding of that will of God. Difficult as it is for us to imagine, that moment, like every moment, remains open to the will of God—God even now is still active then and there, in a time closed to us as past. Hence, we must patiently endure until God's will is finally, fully done. And when that will is done, then we will see that God indeed is good, that even death cannot separate us from his love.

This is the heart of our hope: until the end of everything, God never does everything God can do. That is why we pray for God's will to be done on earth as it is in heaven. For now, we live in the tense moment between what God has done and what God has yet to do. "*Now* we see through a glass darkly; but *then* face to face" (1 Cor 13:12). This is why the earliest Christians prayed, "Come quickly, Lord Jesus": it was a cry for God to finish what he has started. And so for this little girl, whose name we do not know, we pray for God's will to be done on earth as it is in heaven, and we wait expectantly, confidently for that to happen in the end.

***

In history, God has not yet acted fully—except in the life of Jesus of Nazareth. In him, we have seen already what we do not yet see anywhere else for anyone else. As the writer of Hebrews says: "Now in subjecting all things to [human beings, as promised in Psalm 8], God left nothing outside their control. As it is, we do not yet see everything in subjection to them, *but we do see Jesus*" (Heb 2:8–9a). That is, we do not see human beings in their rightful, promised place. We do not see the world set right. But our hope is that what has already happened to Jesus, what is already true for him as the Last Adam and the head of new creation, will be true of us too in the end. We believe that God already has done everything God can do for Jesus, but not yet for us—and so we live by faith and not by sight.

At first, this may seem like anything but good news. But whatever happens to us, whatever comes or goes in our experience, good or bad, fortunate or unfortunate, we can know God is not through being God yet, not through doing what he eternally purposes to do, and when God's will is finally fully done, all things will be made right. Until then, we must avoid both naiveté and despair. We must resist the temptation to distrust God's goodness, and we must refuse to trust our experiences of the world. When God is all in all, everyone will know what we see already not by sight but by faith. In the meantime, we remain faithful, hoping against hope in a God for whom all things are possible and in whom all things not only have their beginning but also their rightful and joyous end.

CHAPTER SEVEN

Christ's Death Lives in Us

"So then death is at work in us, but life is at work in you."

2 CORINTHIANS 4:12

"When Christ calls a man, he bids him come and die."

DIETRICH BONHOEFFER

L ent always comes at just the right time: just as we are all falling-down drunk with the cares of this life, buzzed out of our minds with never-ending, day-to-day worries. Every year, we need time to sober up, time to get our heads clear and our feet steady under us again. Given the state our routine leaves us in, we need time to prepare ourselves for the unimaginable shock of Good Friday and the even greater shock of Resurrection Sunday. Wonderfully, that is precisely the time the church has given us in the Lenten season.

Over the season's forty days, we have the chance to pull ourselves together. With whatever measure of faith has been graced to us, we have the chance to get ourselves ready for what's to come. We have the chance to give ourselves with renewed energy and

45

seriousness to fasting and to almsgiving, to self-denial and to sacrifice. We have the chance to make room for God at the heart of our lives, both by what we give up and by what we give away.

During Lent, we not only fast occasional meals, familiar luxuries, and shallow entertainments. (We're not doing this for self-improvement or our health, after all.) Like Christians have been doing for the beginning, we fast from hasty words and needless chatter, from contemptuous and mistrustful thoughts, from angry and bitter feelings. We fast from unwarranted judgments about ourselves and about others. We give up self-hate. We give up impatience with our children. We give up fear of strangers and hatred of our enemies. And we give away food to the hungry, drink to the thirsty, clothes to the naked, shelter to the homeless. We visit the sick and the imprisoned. We bury the dead with honor. We offer instruction to the ignorant, counsel to the doubting, comfort to the sorrowful, reproof to the erring. We forgive those who have wronged us, and bear with those who trouble and annoy us. We pray for everyone and everything.

* * *

After his baptism and before his temptation in the wilderness, Jesus fasted for forty days. He fasted not to provide an example, but to make it possible for our fasting to work good in us. He fasted so our fasts need not be merely religious. As we live the Lenten season in the spirit of Jesus's fast, we find we are being put in touch with our real (as opposed to our imagined) needs, and with our absolute (as opposed to our conditional) neediness. We also find ourselves being made increasingly aware of our neighbors and their needs, needs that—we suddenly realize—are simply more important than our own.

Lenten spirituality, we might say, is one of the moods of contemplation. It is a heavy mood, and painted in dark hues. By grace, Lent reminds us that we are *creatures*, that our lives are not our own, and moves us into the kind of prayer that this realization makes possible. The truth is, we exist only because God calls us into and upholds us in existence. As Scripture says, it is in him that we live, move, and have our being. As Robert Jenson has said, if for some reason, and against all possibility, God were to decide right now that we are no longer worth sustaining, we would immediately cease to be. And what is more, we would never have been.

By grace, Lent reminds us that we are *dying* creatures, that we are nothing more than dust—strangely animated and self-aware dust, to be sure, but dust nonetheless. On Ash Wednesday, especially, as the poet Cheryl Lawrie says, "Our egos and esteem are held up/to the brutal mirror of the finite." Lawrie call us to come to terms with the fact that in the imposition of ashes, we suffer a hard reminder: "Know that you will end/The world will continue without you." In the words of the prayer books, "From dust you are, and to dust you shall return" (cf. Gen 3:19).

We need not make friends with death, but we do have to come to terms with the fact that we're not going to get out of life alive. In my friend Jason Goroncy's wise words:

> . . . death may indeed be, in some sense, life's enemy. But it's an enemy that, like the strange promise of resurrection, appears to be woven into the warp and woof of life and so of ministry in God's world. And whereas it sometimes may be an enemy from which to flee; at other times it may be the enemy we must embrace as an expression of love's final hope.

By grace, Lent reminds us that we are *sinful* creatures, that we are going to need, again and again, throughout the course of our lives, to be forgiven and reconciled.

We find it difficult, if not impossible, to hear this truth rightly. We almost always hear talk of sin as a *moral* judgment. We imagine that admitting we're sinners is an acknowledgment that we've had bad thoughts, that we've done bad things. But that misses the mark entirely. We are called not to be moral (by the standards and orders of our society) but to be *holy* (as God is holy). Sin, therefore, is not the failure to live a good, clean life but the refusal to let God's goodness come alive in us for the good of others. Sin is whatever stifles or frustrates the fullness of joy in our neighbor's life. Sin is the unwillingness to take the risks that loving our enemies requires. Sin is anything and everything that is done unlovingly, anything and everything that is done in bad faith, anything and everything that leaves us hopeless. As St Paul says, "whatever is not of faith is sin" (Rom 14:23).

I had a dream recently in which several friends and I decided, during a church service, to share our worst faults and offenses with one another. One by one, we took turns giving voice to our inward ugliness. But as we shared, I had this growing sense that something was terribly wrong with what we were doing. And, just as I realized it, a pastor stepped forward and called everyone to pray a blessing over me. That dream reminded me that there's all the difference in the world between exposing my faults and confessing my sins.

Of course, we almost certainly do not know our faults as well as we think we do. But without question we do not know our *sins* as well as we think we do—especially those sins that most seriously grieve God and that most deeply wound our neighbors. We need God to make us aware of them in his time as it is good for us. As Hauerwas says, Only God's favor makes it possible for us to know and acknowledge our sins. Knowing that we've sinned and how we've sinned is already a beginning of salvation.

Lent may be heavy and dark, but it is not dour or hopeless. Above all, by grace, the season reminds us that we are *beloved* creatures. And without that realization, we cannot pray faithfully. Lent is not about my creaturely mortality and sinfulness considered on their own terms. Lent is about what happens to my creaturely mortality and sinfulness as they are assumed by Christ and transfigured, taken up into the divine life and made holy with God's own holiness. God would rather not be God at all than to be God without us. In Christ, therefore, God has taken our creatureliness, our mortality, and our sinfulness as his own. Precisely as the sinful, dying creatures that we are, we are loved. And precisely as the sinful, dying creatures we are, we are called in the Beloved, Jesus, to enjoy God and to work with him for the good of the world.

Sharing in God's work means living Christ's death and letting Christ's death live in us. This is the lesson Lent teaches, and what contemplation makes possible. And it's a defining theme in the writings of St Paul. Take, for example, what he says in Colossians: "for you have died, and your life is hidden with Christ in God" (3:4). Or what he says in Romans: "all of us who have been baptized into Christ Jesus were baptized into his death" (6:3). In 2 Corinthians 2:14–16, he expresses the theme in one of his most difficult, haunting images:

> But thanks be to God, who in Christ always leads us in triumphal procession, and through us spreads in every place the fragrance that comes from knowing him. For we are the aroma of Christ to God among those who are being saved and among those who are perishing; to the one a fragrance from death to death, to the other a fragrance from life to life. Who is sufficient for these things?

Here, Paul seems to have in mind a Roman triumph—the triumphant celebratory parade through the capitol after an emperor or general had won a great victory. In these moments, the entire city would gather to celebrate, welcoming the victorious leader and his troops with flowers and incense, songs and dances. The troops would bring in their train all the treasures they had claimed, and all the prisoners they had captured, prisoners now shamed in defeat and doomed to a life of slavery or death. Startlingly, Paul imagines himself and his ministry team as *God's* captives, spectacularly paraded in a triumphal march before the world, the stench of death—*Christ's* death—heavy on them, "the aroma of Christ" their only glory. Paul returns to this image in 2 Corinthians 4:8–12:

> We are afflicted in every way, but not crushed; perplexed, but not driven to despair; persecuted, but not forsaken; struck down, but not destroyed; always carrying in the body the death of Jesus, so that the life of Jesus may also be made visible in our bodies. For while we live, we are

always being given up to death for Jesus' sake, so that the life of Jesus may be made visible in our mortal flesh. So death is at work in us, but life in you.

***

On Ash Wednesday, we have our faces marked with ashes in the shape of a cross, signifying that we are both-at-once sinners for whom Christ died and saints who have died with him. This ashen cross reverses the first mark we read about in Scripture, the mark God put on Cain. Having murdered his brother, Abel, in a jealous rage, Cain is met with a curse, and he cries out to God in protest (Gen 4:13–16):

> "My punishment is greater than I can bear! Today you have driven me away from the soil, and I shall be hidden from your face; I shall be a fugitive and a wanderer on the earth, and anyone who meets me may kill me." Then the LORD said to him, "Not so! Whoever kills Cain will suffer a sevenfold vengeance." And the LORD put a mark on Cain, so that no one who came upon him would kill him. Then Cain went away from the presence of the LORD, and settled in the land of Nod, east of Eden.

We continue to live in a world "east of Eden," a world in which brother turns against brother, fathers turn against sons, strangers turn against strangers, and neighbors turn against neighbors—a world of unbroken cycles of violence and unbreakable systems of injustice. But we live in the midst of that very world as the Body of the once dead, now risen Christ. Cain fled *from* the Lord's presence, marked by God for his protection. We go out into this world *as* the Lord's presence, and the mark on our bodies proclaims we are already dead.

Christ's death is alive in us; therefore, we can, again and again, in ways conscious and unconscious, die to ourselves. We can die to our ambitions. We can die to our judgments. We can die to our fears. We can die to our prejudices. We can die to our rights. We can die to our common sense. The wonder of it is we find ourselves just by losing ourselves. We "come alive" just in the experience of dying to ourselves. "Death is at work in us" to be sure. We are, as St Paul says, "always being given up to death for Jesus's sake" (2 Cor 4:11). But just so, life is at work in others. And to be dead with Christ is to be hidden in his embrace of the Father, at home in the very heart of God.

CHAPTER EIGHT

What Happens with Those
God Loves

"Lord, he whom you love is ill."

JOHN 11:3

Jesus's story, unlike all other historical events, did not simply
or merely happen at a particular moment to certain people.
Because of who he is, the story of Jesus continues to happen to
all of us, enfolding us in its happening in anticipation of the final
happening that carries creation into its fullness in God. A Gospel
reading, like the story of Lazarus being raised from the dead, does
not merely *report* something Jesus once did for one man and his
sisters. In John's telling, therefore, Lazaraus's story *performs* for
us the here-and-now coming of Jesus. As we read in faith and in
hope, the very same Jesus who presented himself to the characters
in this story re-presents himself to us. Lazarus's friend is also our
contemporary.

As readers of this Gospel from Origen to the present day
have noted, John's stories are made to work as master-parables for
the life of faith. Even the minutest details in these stories (think,

for example, of the woman leaving her bucket at the well or the man by the pool taking up his mat after he is healed) are mysteriously freighted with significance. Lazarus, called back to life but still bound in his grave clothes, figures for us what Romans 8 describes as the conflict of "flesh" and "Spirit." Even after we have been baptized into Christ's death and filled with the Spirit of his new-creation life, we remain bound by the "grave clothes" of the old humanity ("Adam"). Long after we are delivered from slavery in Egypt, we find that we still engage the world as slaves. We are delivered from death not only to life-with-God but also life-with-neighbor. We are saved not *from* one another, but *for* and *to* one another. And so continually we have to have our minds renewed, our hearts purged, our imaginations sanctified, our loves reordered. We have continually to be converted not only to Christ, but also to Lazarus.

***

John Chrysostom, commenting on the story of Lazarus, observed that "many are offended when they see any of those who are pleasing to God suffering anything terrible." Yet the hard truth is that those who are "dear to God" are no more exempted from the sorrows of this life than are non-believers. Nor would they want to be, Still, now, no less than then, it is a hard truth to hear that someone we love—and someone we know loves God and is loved by God—is ill. We inevitably find ourselves asking some form of this question: why does an all-powerful, all-good God allow any evil or suffering at all? If God in fact does love us, and if, as my eight-year-old son puts it, God "has it in him" to keep us from sorrow, then why is anyone ever ill or in trouble? There is, in short, no good answer for us to give to that question. We can offer no adequate theodicy, no righteous justification for God. Instead, we have to live with what we have received: the hope that when all is said and done, God will show himself to be worthy of our confidence. Until then, we pray and we wait. We pray the prayer of the *prophets*—"How long, Lord?"—and the prayer of the *apostles*—"Come quickly, Jesus."

Above all, we pray the prayer of *Jesus*— "Father, let your will be done on earth as it is in heaven."

As with the blindness of the man in John 9, so with Lazarus's terminal illness—and with all illnesses and disease in all times and places: it is "for God's glory." But this does *not* mean that God first imposes illness so that he can later dramatically heal it. God's work does not need to be staged for effect, and God never needs to rely on tricks of timing to demonstrate his power. Illness—disease or suffering of any kind—is what happens in a world gone wrong, a world in which God is willing that his will *not* be done, at least not all-at-once. And yet it's precisely that kind of world in which God's will can be done mercifully and redemptively. God's glory, then, is made known only as there is truly a *need* for mercy and *time* for redemption to take shape.

***

To say that all illness/disease is for God's glory also does not mean that God is glorified by our need for him. God does not need our weakness to make his strength obvious. He does not need darkness for his light to be visible. God needs *nothing*, not even our neediness. We cannot remind ourselves too often of this truth: God does not stand out in comparison to any creaturely reality because God, as creator, is not in competition with creaturely reality.

Finally, to say that all illness/disease is for God's glory does not mean that God is glorified in the power displayed in meeting our need. It is not as if God has abilities that he needs to showcase, powers that he needs to show off. God is not a conqueror but "more than a conqueror"—altogether beyond any and all comparison and just so beyond any and all conflict. Only because divine strength is not the opposite of human weakness can it be perfected *in* that weakness. This is why Jesus says to the disciples that he is glad for their sake that Lazarus has died: "Lazarus isn't asleep. He's dead. And for your sake, I'm glad that I was not there to keep him from dying. After I have awakened him from his sleep—or, as you think of it, after I have raised him from the dead—your eyes will be opened to what you'd never have noticed otherwise." As Augustine says, "Lazarus has to die so that when he is raised the disciples' faith might be raised with him."

Again and again, John's Gospel confronts us with ironic misunderstandings. Here, the disciples—like the master of the wedding feast (John 2), Nicodemus (John 3), the woman at the well (John 4), the man born blind (John 9), as well as the Pharisees and "the Jews" (John 6–9)—misunderstand Jesus's words and actions. And yet, in a doubling of the irony, the disciples' *misapprehension* is in some ways truer than their *apprehension* would have been. When they think that Lazarus is only asleep, they cannot imagine why Jesus is worried for Lazarus. Their incredulity at Jesus's concern is unmistakable: "Lord, if he has fallen asleep, he will be alright" (John 11:12). But when they realize that Lazarus is in fact *dead*, they panic. Their faith is so weak, their fear of death so strong, that they are sure they are going to their own deaths by following Jesus to Bethany. Their feelings move further away from the truth as their understanding comes to a better grasp of the facts.

As Rowan Williams has said, in this story we find Christ on trial. Martha and then her sister Mary face him with the same protest: "if you had been here, Jesus, our brother would not have died." "The Jews," too, wonder why, if he can save others, he does not save Lazarus, whom he so obviously loved. Strikingly, Jesus does not defend himself. And he does not silence the questions that arise. He simply asks them to take him to the tomb: "where have you laid him?" And they respond: "come and see" (11:34), a phrase that recalls other moments in the Gospel, including Jesus's invitation to his first disciples (1:39), Nathanael's call to Philip (1:46), and the Samaritan woman's call to the people of the city (4:29). Jesus does indeed follow them, showing that he has come not only to welcome us into his reality—"I go to prepare a place for you"—but also comes to be welcomed into our reality, however dark, however cold. In this, Jesus reveals the sacred heart of godliness, the beauty of God radiating from a human life. To quote Williams again:

Saints are people who don't silence us, but let us speak
out of what is most real to us, even if it's painful, even
if it's challenging. A saint is somebody who says to you,
"You have God's permission to be yourself, even if that
means pouring out the anger, misery, guilt, confusion."
And a saint is somebody who says, "Let me come with
you to where it hurts." A saint is someone who says,
"Trust and you will see what you never imagined," because the saints in the Church are above all the people
who give us hope, the people who show us that things
can be different, that humanity doesn't have to work in
a sort of cyclical, miserable reworking of resentment,
unhappiness, and selfishness. Saints break that open and
they tell us, "Trust God and God alone knows what you
will see in his world, and what you will see of him."

Meeting Martha's grief, Jesus assures her by identifying himself: "I am the resurrection and the life" (11:25). We might say, as
St Augustine does, that he is the resurrection because he is the life.
But it is no less true that the life he promises us is the life *of resurrection*—and so a life that comes on the far side of death. He is our
life because he is the resurrection; in other words, God does not
save us *from* death but *through* it. Jesus is the answer to his own
question, which he put to Ezekiel: "Mortal, can these bones live?"
This is why he can promise Martha that those who believe in him
"even though they die . . . never die." Just as darkness is light to
God, so death is life to him.

Like the woman at the well returned to Samaria, Andrew returned to his brother, Simon Peter, and Philip had sought out Nathanael and convinced him to come and see Jesus (John 1:35–51),
Martha, having confessed her confidence in Jesus, returns to call
her sister. When Mary goes to him, she kneels at his feet—in recol-
lection of her earlier kneeling to listen to his teaching (Luke 10:39)
and in anticipation of her later kneeling to anoint Jesus's feet with
pure nard in preparation for his death and burial (John 12:1–7). In
this, she models for us the heart of faith.

Jesus, John tells us, is "deeply moved" and begins to weep.
But why is he so moved? Why does he weep, knowing what he is

about to do for Lazarus, for Martha and Mary, for "the Jews," for the disciples? John does not tell us, and so we are left to wonder. Obviously, we know he does not weep because Lazarus is dead. It may be, as many have contended, that he is agitated by the unbelief of those who have gathered at the tomb, but that can only be true in the sense that he pities them. It would seem that he does not weep merely to show that he is human (although of course, as many of the church fathers observed, his tears do reveal the depth of his humanity). And I would argue that he does not weep merely to show us how to grieve (although, as Chrysostom suggests, his weeping shows that weeping for the dead is not inherently faithless and ungodly). Be that as it may, even if we cannot finally say what moved Jesus to tears, we can be sure that Jesus weeps because he is taking into himself human experience in its fullness. As Rowan Williams has said, Christ carries our grief in his love. Later in the Gospel (20:11), Mary Magdalene weeps at Jesus's tomb, revealing that Jesus has entered so fully into the human reality that he knows both what it is to weep and what it is to be wept for, what it is to grieve and what it is to be grieved. His identification with us is absolute and entire, encompassing not only our life but also our death. What is ours, he takes as his own so that what is his, we may receive as our own.

Even though Martha believes in Jesus and trusts his promise to raise her brother from the dead, her protest—"Lord, there is a stench!" (11:39)—shows that she (like Alyosha in Dostoyevsky's *Brothers Karamazov*) cannot suppress her fear and disgust at what death has done to her brother. We should not fault her for it. Jesus doesn't. He simply reminds her of the promise: "you will see the glory of God." In truth, we should be wary of the naïveté that disguises itself as "faith," because it deadens us to the realities of our mortal existence. But we should also be wary of any kind of despair disguised as "realism," because it deadens us to the presence and the promises of God. Either way, it strips us of our humanity and renders us incapable of seeing—or being seen as—the glory of God.

I never read this story without thinking of Franz Wright's "The Raising of Lazarus," and, especially, the ending lines, which capture the shock and horror and wonder and bewilderment that must have descended on everyone that day:

> Peter looked across at Jesus
> with an expression that seemed to say
> You did it, or What have you done?
> And everyone saw
> how their vague and inaccurate
> life made room for his once more.

The ambiguity of that last "his" is perfect. Does it refer to Lazarus? To Jesus? And why is the life of the onlookers "vague and inaccurate"? Because they have not yet learned how to live the life they've been given? Because they have yet to die, and so cannot know what their lives mean? Because they have not yet figured their response to the gospel that Christ forces on them? The answer, I think, to all of these questions is "Yes." This is a Gospel story; therefore, it is about both Jesus and Lazarus—to make room for one is to make room for the other. And the Gospel makes clear that the only way to live an accurate life—to live truthfully, accessibly—is through radical identification with Jesus in his care for our neighbors. As his disciples, impossibly saved from death, we have to join him in his journey to where it hurts most We have to roll away the gravestone from our lives and the lives of our neighbors—even if that means we expose a deep corruption. We have to make room in our lives for Christ to call the dead to life so that we can take up in his Spirit the work of stripping away the "grave clothes" that bind them to their past. We should have no illusions: not everyone will rejoice in what we do. And we won't always take joy in it ourselves. But like Thomas and the other disciples, like Martha and Mary and "the Jews," all we have to do is show up where Jesus is—and wait for him to do what only he can do.

CHAPTER NINE

Turning from God for God's Sake

"Leave your gift at the altar . . ."

MATTHEW 5:24

"Fasting is better than prayer . . . almsgiving better than both."

CLEMENT OF ROME

Not all religion is good religion. If, as St James says, good religion is care for widows and orphans, then there must be *bad* religion, religion that cares nothing for those most in need because it is solely consumed with itself. St Paul warns us it is possible to have faith that moves mountains and to give our bodies to be burned and still not to be living and dying in love. And that kind of religion—even when deeply felt and rigorously practiced—is simply worthless: it is self-serving, self-determined, self-glorifying. In spite of appearances and protests to the contrary—"Lord, Lord, did we not . . ."—it ultimately has nothing to do either with God or with grace, and does nothing to transform us into the Christlikeness for which we are made.

In a stunning word, no less powerful now than when it was first given millennia ago, the prophet Isaiah, speaking for YHWH, condemns such bad religion in the starkest terms (58:5–10):

> Is such the fast that I choose, a day to humble oneself? Is it to bow down the head like a bulrush, and to lie in sackcloth and ashes? Will you call this a fast, a day acceptable to the LORD? Is not this the fast that I choose: to loose the bonds of injustice, to undo the thongs of the yoke, to let the oppressed go free, and to break every yoke? Is it not to share your bread with the hungry, and bring the homeless poor into your house; when you see the naked, to cover them, and not to hide yourself from your own kin? Then your light shall break forth like the dawn, and your healing shall spring up quickly . . . .

God is no less clear about what good religion requires than he is about what bad religion entails: "remove the yoke from among you, the pointing of the finger, the speaking of evil . . . [and then] offer your food to the hungry and satisfy the needs of the afflicted." Just so, the divine light shall rise in the darkness, so that all will flourish in mutual blessing.

We may summarize Isaiah's prophetic vision in this way: piety does not please God; only charity does. Whatever good they do for us, and however crucial they are for our witness to others, we do God no favors with our songs, our prayers, our fasts, our offerings, our sermons. He has no need of gifts from us, even if he delights in receiving them when they are offered faithfully. It is for our own good and the good of others that he calls us to offer our bodies as living sacrifices. He delights in us clothing the naked, feeding the hungry, visiting the sick and the imprisoned—so long as we do it in love. He delights in us welcoming strangers into our homes and sharing meals with our enemies—so long as we do it in love. He wants us lovingly to "break every yoke"—doing all we can (in his power, not our own) to free others from whatever oppresses them—because that is when we are being what he has created us to be.

This call to serve the poor—that is, anyone in need and within reach of our care—is at the heart of the life of faith. If, as St John puts it, the love of God is alive in us, then our religion matters less to us than does our neighbor's need. Cyprian of Carthage, in the spirit of Isaiah, warns us that "prayer without almsgiving is barren." To that end, we have to "fast" even from our religion, our spirituality, in order to "taste" the suffering of others. This is the essence of the Eucharist event, which makes us to share in the sufferings of Christ and his sacrifice for the life of the world.

I don't mean to suggest that God hates our worship or that care for others is all there is to the life of faith, of course. The Christian life is a life of movements, a life that Jürgen Moltmann describes as breathing: we inhale in worship and then exhale in witness the very life of God. Or, in the words of Christoph Blumhardt, every one of us must undergo two conversions: first, from the world to God; then, from God to the world. And these movements do not happen once, one after the other, but at the same time and over the entire course of our lives. As people of faith, we must always be moving both toward God and away from God—always for God's and our neighbor's sake.

We can picture these movements, these conversions, this inhalation and exhalation, by comparing the figures in Fritz Eichenberg's *The Christ of the Breadlines* and David Jones's *Christ Sending Forth the Disciples*.

Notice, all the figures are bowed, even Christ. But some are bowed in desperation, the others in reflection. The former are burdened with need; the latter, with a calling to serve those in need. Christ shares both burdens, just as he stands in both lines—at the head of one, and in the midst of the other. He is both source of the life of good religion, and its guide. We care for others in him. And in going out from him we find him again in "the least of these."

Worship—and in particular, the Eucharist—marks the turn of these movements. Every week, at the table, we find ourselves drawn to Christ by his Father and driven out by his Spirit. We come to church just because those pressures—that pull, that push—carry us in and carry us out like the tides. No one has seen this more clearly or said it more forcefully than Mother Maria of Paris:

> It would be a great lie to tell those who are searching: "Go to church, because there you will find peace." The opposite is true. The Church tells those who are at peace and asleep: "Go to church, because there you will feel real anguish for your sin and the world's sin. There you will feel an insatiable hunger for Christ's truth. There, instead of becoming lukewarm, you'll be set on fire; instead of being pacified, you'll become alarmed; instead of learning the wisdom of this world, you will become fools for Christ."

* * *

We must hear this call to turn from God for God's sake as a word of gospel, not law. It is a word of permission and possibility, not demand or judgment. Because Christ is risen and ascended, because he is in us and we are in him, because his Spirit rests on us as we rest in his Father, we may turn from God to the world both for God's sake and the world's. In fact, because God is the living God, turning *from* him is just another way of turning *to* him. With that realization in mind, we are freed to engage the difficult, never-ending work of caring for those in need in hope, not optimism; in faith, not idealism; in love, not ambition.

In Isaiah's prophesy, God promises not only to provide for us, but also that we will ourselves *be* the provision—always, of course, in the barren, parched places to which we are called and sent. We know we are not going to "fix" the world, however heroically we try. But we also know that we can do some good for our neighbors, precisely because in them we come face-to-face with the one who is our good.

CHAPTER TEN

Loving Obedience

"For the love of God is this, that we obey his commandments."

1 JOHN 5:3

"This is my commandment, that you love one another
as I have loved you."

JOHN 15:12

It is difficult for Christians in our time and place to know how to
talk about obedience. For one thing, it is easy for us to confuse
all talk about obedience with a call for dominance or subjugation.
For another, it is tempting for us to think of grace and faith as
inherently at odds with obedience, at least in part because we have
been taught, implicitly if not explicitly, to associate obedience with
"works" and "self righteousness." But we *are* called to obedience,
and that means we have to find some way to talk intelligibly about
what it means to obey.

As always, we must begin and end with Christ. First and fore-
most, he said he obeyed by doing what he saw the Father doing,

so we know obedience is godly attentiveness to what God wants for us and for others in a given moment. This attentiveness, this tuned-in-ness, makes us (as John Ruysbroek says) "ready and supple" to participate with the Spirit's work in the world.

From careful attention to Christ's life as the Scriptures reveal it, we also learn that obedience isn't a necessary evil, much less inimical to our integrity as creatures. Instead, obedience is the form creaturely freedom necessarily takes. We don't obey *instead* of living in freedom, and we don't obey *until* we earn our freedom. Freedom simply is *in* obedience and obedience is *in* freedom. As Rowan Williams says, "To submit to God is to be most directly in touch with what is most real. To refuse that submission is not to be free of an alien violence but to become an alien to yourself."

We cannot reimagine obedience without reimagining power, as well. And God's power is not coercive or violent. Indeed, God, as creator, cannot do violence any more than he can lie. God does not overpower or defeat, does not forcefully overcome resistances. God has no opposites or equals; hence, divine power has no obstacles to its fulfillment. God does not have to overcome or defeat any resisting powers; after all, the only realities that exist do so at the mercy of God. There is only God and everything that God creates and holds in being; therefore, for God to get his will done he has only to will it: no struggle against rival powers or victory over enemies is necessary.

To be sure, we *need* God to be powerful. We begin truly to discover this need through our experiences of power and powerpowerlessness, especially death. And we need that power to be absolute. Otherwise, our existence as creatures is not sheer grace, and we have no ground for our hope in God's promises, and in particular the promise to raise us from the dead. But that very neediness works against us. We can invent for ourselves and/or impose on others ways of living with God that lead to us imagining that God's power is at our disposal, for our use, and/or that God's power is a looming threat.

If we're going to have our imaginations of God's power converted, then we're going to have to look to Christ. Only in him are

God's being-act and creaturely powers perfectly at-one-ed. This is why we trust not *our* experiences with God, but *Jesus's*.

What do we discover when we look to Jesus to see God's power? We see that God's power is radically unlike both our power and our powerlessness, our strength and our weakness. God's power is revealed in the virgin birth and the resurrection, and especially in the forgiveness of sins and the transfiguration of sinners. We understand nothing yet in the light of the gospel until we grasp that God's power is revealed most completely for us in the weakness of the cross.

That is, we start to realize the character of God's power only in our experiences of weakness that bring us into communion with God's "weakness." God's power/weakness sustains where we wish it would deliver, and delivers when we wish it would sustain. St Paul reveals this truth to us in a difficult, if familiar, passage: "I will boast all the more gladly of my weaknesses, so that the power of Christ may dwell in me. Therefore, I am content with weaknesses, insults, hardships, persecutions, and calamities for the sake of Christ; for whenever I am weak, then I am strong" (2 Cor 12:9–10). In one of his letters from prison, Bonhoeffer articulates this same truth in heartbreaking terms:

> There is nothing that can replace the absence of someone dear to us, and one should not even attempt to do so. One must simply hold out and endure it. At first that sounds very hard, but at the same time it is also a great comfort. For to the extent the emptiness truly remains unfilled one remains connected to the other person through it. It is wrong to say that God fills the emptiness. God in no way fills it but much more leaves it precisely unfilled and thus helps us preserve—even in pain—the authentic relationship. Further more, the more beautiful and full the remembrances, the more difficult the separation. But gratitude transforms the torment of memory into silent joy.

God is more concerned for our transformation than with our safety. And God can afford to sustain us until we are transformed because God is not afraid for us. Nothing can resist his will for us: "what can separate us from the love of God?" In sum, then, we face and overcome all resistance to God's will in our lives by simple reliance upon the power that knows no resistance and so does not need to overcome anything to be itself. Obedience, therefore, is not the breaking of our will by a more powerful will; obedience is the healing of our will by participation in its source. In the words of John Webster:

> Listening means obedience, and obedience is not craven submission; it's not born of fear. Obedience to God is the lifelong task of giving my consent to the shape which God has for my life. Obedience is letting God put me in the place where I can be the sort of person I am made by God to be.

***

Henry Ossawa Tanner's painting *The Banjo Lesson* (1893) shows what a "listening obedience" is like. The young child, just learning to play, cannot even hold the instrument with ease. But the teacher embraces him and holds the banjo, leaving room for the boy to stand on his own, and allowing him to play by himself. Neither one looks at or even seems aware of the other. Both the boy and the man attend to the instrument, their attentions fused in the effort of making the song.

No doubt, as this child grows physically and skillfully, the master will give him even more room. And their attentions will continue to fuse, more and more tightly, until the student knows all that the master knows.

In much the same way, as we go from faith to faith, learning to obey more fully, our attention increasingly fused with God's, we find ourselves obeying without self-regard. In the wisdom of the prophet Isaiah (30:20–21):

> Though the LORD may give you the bread of adversity and the water of affliction, yet your Teacher will not hide himself any more, but your eyes shall see your Teacher.

> And when you turn to the right or when you turn to the
> left, your ears shall hear a word behind you, saying, "This
> is the way; walk in it."

Following Christ, then, is listening raptly to a teacher's voice, a teacher who hides behind us, so to speak, making room for us to "play" on our own.

***

But what does this mean? What does Christ command us to do? And how does his command come to us? It comes to us via the Spirit's illumination of the way of life Jesus embodies, a way of life described in the Sermon on the Mount.

The Sermon on the Mount is law: it is given to us to obey. And the same goes for the Ten Commandments. But these are *Christ's* law—and so come to us not as a series of discrete directives but as articulations of the one command to love our neighbor, the command that fulfills the whole law. We do not and cannot obey Christ by effort or even by intention—only by absorption in wonder at him and his life, which the Sermon and the Ten Commandments describe. When we read the Sermon or hear the Commandments, we should hear them always only as rhapsody to the beauty of Jesus the Galilean, Mary's son and God's revelation. We should be absorbed in the music of the Sermon in a self-forgetting way, totally without regard for our keeping or failing to keep it. Instead, our eyes are fixed on Jesus and the wonder of his life lived for others.

***

If in one sense we obey Christ by attending to the wonder of his life lived for us, in another sense we join in his obedience as we attend with him to the wonder of his Father's love for him and for us. Or to say it slightly different, as we contemplate the glory of the Father, Christ's obedience begins to happen in us. Where there is wonder for Christ that opens out on wonder for the Father, there the Spirit is brooding, creating new life.

Saying it in this way brings us close to St John's way of talking about the intimate interweaving of love, obedience, and the commandments. All the commandments, according to John, are summed up in one commandment: love one another as you have been loved. And the fulfillment of that command is simply participation in the very love that is commanded.

"Give what you demand, and command what you will," St Augustine prayed. And we can join him in that prayer, knowing the answer already: God never commands what he doesn't also by that very command give. God's command, after all, is God's own Word, and so every command is a call to be one with that Word, and the call effects what it invites. God summons us to the life he requires of us, and his summons, like Jesus's call to Peter to step out of the boat and come, enables us to do what it requires.

In the same way, God's obedience is also God's own Word, carried out in God's own Spirit. And since Christ's person and work are inseparable, the Son's human response to the Father is taken up into the dynamics of the Triune life—and by the same Spirit we are taken up with it. For that very reason, our obedience is nothing less or other than a share in God's own life with God.

***

We are finally in a position to see *why* God requires obedience. Barth articulates the divine purpose as revealed in the gospel:

> God wants man to be His creature. Furthermore, He wants him to be His partner. There is a *causa Dei* in the world. God wants light, not darkness. He wants cosmos, not chaos. He wants peace, not disorder. He wants man to administer and to receive justice rather than to inflict and to suffer injustice. He wants man to live according to the Spirit rather than according to the flesh. He wants man bound and pledged to Him rather than to any other authority. He wants man to live and not to

die. Because He wills these things God is Lord, Shepherd, and Redeemer of man, who in His holiness and mercy meets His creature; who judges and forgives, rejects and receives, condemns and saves.

Why, then does God call us to obey? Because that is simply the form the *causa Dei* takes as it comes into our lives. God does not require obedience to test us, but to train us, to transform us, to fit us to his own life. God requires obedience not to break us but to make us, to fill us up with his own kenotic glory. In a word, "obedience" is just another way of saying "salvation by grace."

CHAPTER ELEVEN

The Needs of God

"Jesus, tired out from his journey, ..."

JOHN 4:6

At one level, it comes as no surprise that Jesus is tired. He is, after all, truly human. And yet, there is serious theological depth in this seemingly insignificant detail. Jesus calls those who are weary and overburdened to come to him for rest (Matt 11:28–30). And he does so as the one who recapitulates human experience, including our weariness, our neediness. Jesus needs rest, too.

As John's Gospel tells it, Jesus's encounter with a Samaritan woman at Jacob's Well re-enacts Israel's temptation at Meribah (Exod 17; Ps 95). When we read Israel's story through John's re-telling of it, we are positioned to see what is happening with us, here-and-now. "For whatever was written in former days was written for our instruction . . ." (Rom 15:4). How can this be? Because Jesus re-lives the human experience, re-enlivening it with the very life of God. What he does as Israel-in-person, he does for each and all. In his own person, he brings the rest of God into communion with the weariness of humanity, so that in that communion death is overcome with life, and darkness is dispelled by light. In him, wandering is transformed into journeying.

At Rephidim, Israel had no water to drink, and so they protested and complained against Moses (Exod 17:1–7). "Why did you bring us out of Egypt to let us die in this desert?" But where Israel quarreled with Moses, Jesus graciously asks for a drink. His thirst, unlike theirs, does not drive him to anger or imprecation. Israel could not trust Moses—or the God of Moses—to care for them in their need. Jesus, however, as Israel-in-person, entrusts himself to the care of a stranger—a Samaritan woman, no less. He puts himself at her mercy just so that in the end he can have mercy on her.

That is always the way of God with us. In the life of Jesus, God—impassible, unassailable, unapproachable in power, absolutely unconditioned by any reality outside his own life—makes himself vulnerable and dependent upon us. The creator assumes creation and the infinite one assumes finitude. The one who is life itself, takes on mortality. The one who has no need, makes himself needy. And he does so just for our sake and for our good.

Think of how often this happens in the Gospels. Not only in the womb of Mary, but also in the home of Joseph. Not only in the waters of baptism, but also at the table of his friends and his enemies. He asks the disciples to pray with him in the garden. He allows a woman to wash his feet with her tears in the Pharisee's house. He does not carry his own cross.

Christ continues even now to make himself needy for us. "God thirsts that we may thirst for him" (*Catechism of the Catholic Church*, 2560). As Maximus Confessor says in his *Centuries*, Christ wants to be conceived as a child in each of us according to the strength of our desire for God. Jesus wants to be as dependent on us as he was on Mary, the God-bearer. Only in that way is his character truly formed in us. As we sanctify him in our hearts (1 Pet 3:15), we find we are the ones being made holy with God's own divine-human holiness. As we strive to speak lovingly to God about others and about God to others, we find we are ourselves being made true and loving. As we pray, and inevitably find ourselves failing, we are caught up into God's own intercession for us. As we care for those most in need, we find that we are ourselves receiving the grace we know we need but cannot summon for or offer to ourselves.

Scripture promises that "we have peace with God through our Lord Jesus Christ, through whom we have obtained access to this grace in which we stand" (Rom 5:2). But how have we obtained this access? How does Christ win it for us? Not by changing the Father's will toward us. And not by providing us with an example that shows the possibility of living a better life. He secures this access into grace for us ontologically, by changing the very nature of creaturely existence. As Maximus the Confessor put it, Christ's human life, death, and resurrection is the "remedy" for all that corrupts creation. Through his "flesh" God restores human nature (and so the nature of all things) to a state of grace. But not merely restores—*makes new*. What is assumed is not only healed but also filled with the Spirit, brought into the fullness of God. Christ does not open the way back to Eden. Christ opens the way into the life of God.

The Epistle also reminds us that we hope to "share in the glory of God" (Rom 5:2)—the very God who identifies himself as the one who does not share his glory with another (Isa 42:8)! How can this be? Just because, in Christ, we in fact are not another. We are flesh of his flesh, bone of his bone, his joint-heirs and co-operants. What is his is ours. What happens to him, happens to us. Nothing that the Father means for him is not also meant for us. Everything the Spirit does for him is also done for us. In the words of Paul, "God's love"—the Father's love for the Son and the Son's love for the Father, as well as their love for creation—"has been poured into our hearts through the Holy Spirit that has been given to us" (Rom 5:5).

***

The Gospel of John has a remarkably strange accounting of time. The past and the future are present in ways we'd never expect.

"Before Abraham was, I am" (John 8:58), Jesus says, and leaves everyone in confusion. And prior to his crucifixion, he prays, "I glorified you on earth by finishing the work that you gave me to do. So now, Father, glorify me in your own presence with the glory that I had in your presence before the world existed" (John 17:4–5). In his epistle to the Romans, Paul insists that Christ died "at the right time for the ungodly" (Rom 5:6). And he then immediately makes clear that this "right time" is the moment of our weakness, the moment of our estrangement from God and enmity against God. God proves the authenticity of his love by coming just when we cannot be thought to deserve it.

John's Gospel, in turn, shows that the one who comes at the right time, in the fullness of time (Gal 4:4), is the one who brings all things with him into his "hour" (John 12:20–26), the moment of his strength, the moment of his triumph over evil and death, the moment in which he estranges us from all estrangement by bringing us into his oneness with the Father. The one who is in the embrace of the Father (John 1:18) has gone to prepare a place for us, that where he is, we may be too (John 14:3). "God makes all things beautiful in his time" (Eccl 3:11). How does he do that? By drawing us into Christ's "hour," so that his beautification beautifies us as well.

"Jesus said to her, 'Go, call your husband'" (John 4:16). It is easy to infer from the woman's confession that she has no husband that this woman has had a tumultuous and scandalous sexual history. St Augustine, for example, suggests that after all her husbands she has finally taken up with an illicit lover. But of course we do not know why or how her story played out the way that it did. Perhaps each of her husbands had died, and someone had taken her in pity? Regardless, this reference to marriage cannot be insignificant. Brant Pitre, in his *Jesus the Bridegroom*, suggests that this story is a retelling of Jacob's encounter with Rachel at the well (Gen 29:1–9). In the Gospel's retelling, as Pitre reads it, Jesus, like Jacob, encounters this woman as his bride-to-be. But unlike Rachel, who was a beauty, this woman is not conventionally desirable. She is more like Rachel's undesirable sister, Leah. She is a Samaritan. She has had five husbands. For whatever reason and under whatever conditions, she is now living with a man who is not her husband.

Pitre points out that 2 Kings 17 describes the Samaritans as committing idolatry with five foreign gods, a detail that perhaps informs John's account of this woman's history. Be that as it may, the suggestiveness is wildly scandalous: Jesus—the new Jacob—is seen to be falling for a Samaritan—and one with a questionable history at that! The disciples are astonished for good reason. But that, in a word, *is* the gospel: Christ, our bridegroom, seeks out only the ungodly, sinners, the enemies of God (Rom 5:6–10). God finds us lovely when we are anything but desirable, and in that very finding, he makes us what we otherwise are not and could never be. His desire for us is what makes us desirable. He beautifies us with his confession of love for us.

"What you have said is true" (John 4:17). The events at Meribah (Exod 17:1–7) led to judgment against both Israel and Moses. But Jesus's exchange with the Samaritan leads to a different kind of judgment altogether, a judgment that leads not to death but to life. Jesus reveals the woman's condition precisely by making space for her to confess it in her own words. Just as she says what is true, she opens herself up to the one who is the Truth.

At first, her vision is blurred (like the blind man in Mark 8, who sees people like trees walking). She sees that Jesus is a prophet, but like Nicodemus and so many others in John's Gospel, she has no sense of what that means. Like Israel at Meribah, she fails to realize that the Lord is present. She knows that the Messiah is coming, but does not recognize that he has already come. The same, of course, is true for all of us. It is never *God* who is absent. *We* are the ones who fail to be present. God is not silent. We are the ones who cannot hear what is spoken. Like Jacob, we all have to confess, "Surely the Lord was in this place, and I was unaware of it" (Gen 28:16). Lent is a time for remembering how little we truly understand, how much we have still to learn.

And yet, unlike Israel, the Samaritan woman is open to the presence she does not yet recognize. He is not only the new Jacob, but also the new Moses. Jacob's Well is the burning bush, and so

Christ declares himself to her: "I Am is speaking to you." She suddenly finds herself on holy ground.

"Just then his disciples came" (John 4:27). Precisely in that moment—before we're told a word of her response to Jesus's self-revelation—the disciples return. We should live as if this is always true: we arrive in every moment just after the One Who Is has made himself known. Whomever we encounter, and whenever we encounter them, we already find ourselves having returned to holy ground. Because the I Am is always there before us.

Upon their return, the disciples are astonished to see what is happening, and the questions they have to ask are bad ones. But at least they have enough sense not to say anything. More often than not, that's our greatest evangelistic act: simply not asking the question that comes to mind. As Bonhoeffer says in *Life Together*, the first, and in many ways the most important, ministry we offer to others is the ministry of holding our tongues: "It must be a decisive rule of every Christian fellowship that each individual is prohibited from saying much that occurs to him."

Then "the woman left her water jar" and returned to the town (4:21). The Samaritan leaves her jar just as the other disciples had left their fishing nets, their tax tables, their swords and daggers to follow Jesus. This is surely a sign of what Christ's self-revelation inevitably does to all of us: it disrupts our lives, makes it so that we find ourselves caught up in a strange new world of concerns. Remembering him, we forget everything we once thought important and definitive for our lives. When he lays hold of us, we lose touch with everything that we once grasped so tightly (cf. Phil 3:13–14).

She returns to the city without her water-jar but with an invitation and an inviting question: "Come see someone who told me everything I have ever done. He cannot be the Messiah, can he?" (John 4:29). As Chrysostom says, "winged by joy," this Samaritan woman "performs the office of Evangelists." And "she calls not one or two, as did Andrew and Philip, but having aroused a whole city and people, so brought them to him."

Her witness is harmless as a dove and cunning as a serpent. Chrysostom continues:

Observe here the great wisdom of the woman; she neither declared the fact plainly, nor was she silent, for she
desired not to bring them in by her own assertion, but
to make them to share in this opinion by hearing him
for themselves. . . . Nor did she say, Come, believe but,
Come, see; a gentler expression than the other, and one
more attractive to them. Do you see the wisdom of this
woman? She knew, and knew with certainty, that if they
had only tasted from Jacob's Well, they would be affected
in the same manner as she herself had been.

She was tactful—overjoyed, but neither overeager nor pushy.
With her testimony, she gently created the same space of possibility for her neighbors that Christ had created for her. John says
that many believed on him because of her witness, although they
make it clear to her, "It is no longer because of your words that
we believe, for we have heard for ourselves . . ." (4:41–42a). And,
astonishingly, they come to understand him in a way she had not
even suggested. He is not only Israel's Messiah but the Savior of the
world (4:42b).

We have much to learn from her witness. Not least that our
task is not to convince our neighbors to believe in Jesus, much
less to accept our beliefs and way of life as their own. We need to
remember that our calling is nothing more or less than to bear
witness to what God has done in our lives in ways true to his
character—his humility, his gentleness, his mercy, his patience, his
compassion.

In evangelization, the how and the what are inseparable and
mutually determined. The kindness of God leads to repentance,
Scripture says. So it is only as we kindly bear witness to God's
kindness that we can help others find the way to repentance. We
are at most only midwives: we do not create life in others; we
merely come alongside them to help them give birth to the Christ
the Spirit has formed in them.

CHAPTER TWELVE

How God Becomes Human

"I am again in the pain of childbirth until Christ is formed in you."

GALATIANS 4:19

"We were gentle among you, like a nurse tenderly caring for
her own children"

1 THESSALONIANS 2:7

The good news: Christ will not leave us alone. He is always already present, ever nearer than we imagine—of course differently than we either expect or desire. As a result, we are called not simply to patience but to deep attentiveness. During Advent, especially, we learn again to receive the gifts God wants to give rather than the gifts we've asked to receive, because we know that what God has prepared for us is better by far than anything we could think to ask for ourselves. Advent is a time to attune our awareness to Christ in his "second coming."

Most of us, I'm sure, are accustomed to thinking of only two comings of Christ, the first coming of incarnation and the second coming, which we expect at the end of history. But Bernard of Clairvaux suggests we think instead of *three* comings of Christ:

> We know that there are three comings of the Lord. The third lies between the other two. It is invisible, while the other two are visible. In the first coming he was seen on earth, dwelling among men. . . . In the final coming all flesh will see the salvation of our God, and they will look on him whom they pierced. . . . In his first coming our Lord came in our flesh and in our weakness; in this middle coming he comes in spirit and in power; in the final coming he will be seen in glory and majesty.

What Bernard calls "the intermediate coming" is, he says, always "hidden," one that the elect find within themselves in the experience of contemplation. If he is right, and I am convinced that he is, then *Christ is always coming to us*—meekly, secretly, with graceful awkwardness. Indeed, he comes not so much *to* us as *through* us.

Christ "appears" in this sense only through our *laboring*. He "comes again" and is present to us and to others just as we bring him to bear. In other words, we are not only children of God; we also have to become *theotokoi*—mothers of God. Or to say the same thing another way, we can become like Christ only by first becoming like Mary, his mother.

This is what the apostle Paul models for us in his letter to the Galatians: "My little children, for whom I am again in the pain of childbirth until Christ is formed in you" (4:19). St Paul's labor is like Mary's in that God is being birthed through him. He labors painfully until Christ is formed in them anew. And then he nurses them with the milk of the Word until they are mature.

Paul makes a similar, but perhaps even more provocative claim in Romans: "We know that the whole creation has been groaning in labor pains until now; and not only the creation, but we ourselves, who have the first fruits of the Spirit, groan inwardly while we wait for adoption, the redemption of our bodies" (8:22–23). Here, the entire creation joined with the saints as the body of Christ, is imaged as a mother giving birth to new creation. It is as if Christ himself is in labor. Just as he was born of a woman, taken from her as Abel and Cain were taken from Eve, so he carries new creation in his womb, and it will be taken from his side as Eve was taken from Adam.

***

In his *New Seeds of Contemplation*, Thomas Merton says that the only true joy in life is to escape from the prison of our false self. But so long as we are trying to escape from that prison, so long as we are trying to be our "true self," we are only ever false to our deepest calling; we will be living contrary to the truth of our being. What we need, instead, is a healthy self-forgetfulness—or, better, a holy other-remembrance—a becoming one with the love of God that makes it so that we are not thinking of how we can be our own best selves but how we can attend to and care for those right in front of us who need our mercy and compassion.

If we can become that kind of attentive, if we can be delightfully absorbed in loving our neighbor, if we can be "rapt with divine love," if we can act with the abandon that only God's love makes possible, it is because the life of Jesus is happening in us. That kind of living would mean that we are, in fact, pregnant with Christ. And so, our words and our silences, our expressions and our impressions, our action and our stillness would bespeak him and bring his goodness to bear—all without our knowing it or taking pride in it. Paradoxically, then, we must forget ourselves, and even our relationship with God, to truly be ourselves, to truly be one with the love that has loved us into being. Mothering, after all, is a peculiar kind of attention and care.

***

It may strike you as strange to talk of becoming one with the love of God, and it may seem out-and-out wrong to talk of forgetting ourselves and our relationship with God. But if it does, I suspect that is because so many of us have come to think of God as just one more person in our lives; the most important person, to be sure; but the first among the many, nonetheless. We imagine that loving God is something different from—and at some level in competition with—loving our neighbor, as if God simply takes priority over the neighbor. And we imagine that loving God is easy compared to loving our neighbor. But contemplation teaches us that God saves us from our illusions precisely by throwing us into the care of and responsibility for our neighbor. In the language of 1 John, it is by loving the neighbor whom we can see that we prove—in both senses of the word—that the life of the God whom we cannot see is alive in us. And contemplation teaches us that God is not one more person in our lives: God *is* our life. God is the one in whom we live, move, and have our being. We are not merely with Christ; we are *in* him and he is in us in such a way that we are the temple of the Spirit and the Father is at home in us. As St Paul says, "Set your minds on things that are above, not on things that are on earth, for you have died, and your life is hidden with Christ in God. When Christ who is your life is revealed, then you also will be revealed with him in glory" (Col 3:2–4).

We are hidden with Christ in God—from ourselves, as well as from others. And in this way, we are not so much mothers as yet-to-be-children. We should not think of this as poetry: we are held in our faith in God long before that faith becomes our own. We believe only because others believed for us. And we go on believing only as others go on believing for us and in us. We are carried in the womb of others' faith.

Merton observes that we hate thinking of ourselves as beginners, and yet in the life of faith and prayer we are always only beginners. And Kierkegaard, meditating on the faith of Abraham, remarks that faith comes not at the beginning, easily, but at the far end of life, after much difficulty. Similarly, St Ignatius describes his impending martyrdom not as his death but as his birth. These are the ways we ought to envision Christian maturity: our maturity lies always ahead of us as promised to us; the possibility of full

Christlikeness always drawing us forward into deeper, wider responsibility for those who need our care.

We are not always giving birth to the work of God in others, of course. We are not only like Paul and Mary, but we are also often like Anna: we bear witness to Christ's coming in the world around us, in the lives of our friends and enemies (Luke 2:36–38). And we are often like Elizabeth, Mary's cousin: we provide sanctuary for those who are giving birth to Christ, and we ourselves give birth to that which prepares the way for Christ to come through them (1:39–43). We are midwives and nurses, tenderly caring for others as they give birth and tenderly caring for those who are born in their radical vulnerability. In all of these and other ways, our labor is a share in the groaning of creation to give birth to the new-creation work of God.

List of Books Cited

Augustine of Hippo. *The Confessions*. London: Penguin, 2003.

Balthasar, Hans Urs von. *Theo-Drama V*. San Francisco: Ignatius, 1998.

Barth, Karl. *The Humanity of God*. Louisville: Westminster John Knox, 1960.

Bernard of Clairvaux. *St Bernard's Sermons on the Nativity*. Chulmleigh, UK: Augustine, 1985.

Bonhoeffer, Dietrich. *Letters and Papers from Prison*. Minneapolis: Fortress, 2015.

———. *Life Together*. San Francisco: Harper Collins, 1978.

———. *Sanctorum Communio*. Minneapolis: Fortress, 2009.

Coakley, Sarah. *God, Sexuality, and the Self: An Essay "On the Trinity."* Cambridge: Cambridge University Press, 2013.

Gunton, Colin. *Father, Son, and Holy Spirit: Toward a Fully Trinitarian Theology*. London: T. & T. Clark, 2003.

Eliot, T.S. *Four Quartets*. New York: Houghton Mifflin Harcourt, 2014.

Hart, David Bentley. *The Experience of God: Being, Consciousness, Bliss*. New Haven: Yale University Press, 2013.

Hilary of Poitier. *On the Trinity*. A Select Library of the Nicene and Post-Nicene Fathers of the Christian Church, Second Series. Edited by Philip Schaff, vol. IX. New York: Scribner's, 1890.

Jenson, Robert W. *On Thinking the Human: Resolutions to Difficult Notions*. Grand Rapids: Eerdmans, 2003.

———. *Systematic Theology Vol 2: The Works of God*. New York: Oxford University Press, 2002.

John Chrysostom. *Commentary on Saint John the Apostle and Evangelist: Homilies 1–47*. Fathers of the Church. Washington, DC: Catholic University of America Press, 2000.

Kierkegaard, Søren. *Fear and Trembling*. London: Penguin, 1985.

Lewis, C. S. *The Silver Chair*. Grand Rapids: Zondervan, 2005.

Maximus the Confessor. *St. Maximus the Confessor: Selected Writings*. Classics of Western Spirituality; Mahwah, NJ: Paulist, 1985.

Meister Eckhart. *Meister Eckhart: The Essential Sermons, Commentaries, Treatises and Defense*. Translated by Edmund Colledge and Bernard McGinn. New York: Paulist, 1981.

Merton, Thomas. *Contemplative Prayer*. New York: Image/Doubleday, 1996.

―――. *New Seeds of Contemplation*. New York: New Directions, 2007.

Moltmann, Jürgen. *The Source of Life: The Holy Spirit and the Theology of Life*. Minneapolis: Fortress Press, 1997.

Nicholas of Cusa. *On Learned Ignorance*. Online: http://jasper-hopkins.info/DI-I-12-2000.pdf.

Pieper, Joseph. *Happiness and Contemplation*. South Bend, IN: St Augustine's Press, 1998.

Pitre, Brant. *Jesus the Bridegroom: The Greatest Love Story Ever Told*. New York: Image, 2018.

Skobtsova, Maria. *Essential Writings*. Modern Spiritual Masters. Maryknoll, NY: Orbis, 2002.

Sonderegger, Kate. *Systematic Theology Vol. 1: The Doctrine of God*. Minneapolis: Fortress, 2015.

Stein, Edith. "Ways to Know God." In *Knowledge and Faith*, translated by Walter Redmond. Washington, DC: ICS, 2000.

Teresa of Ávila. *The Way of Perfection*. New Kensington, PA: Whitaker House, 2017.

Thomas Aquinas. *Summa Theologica*. Notre Dame, IN: Ave Maria Press, 2000.

Ware, Kallistos. *The Orthodox Way*. Crestwood, NY: St Vladimir's Seminary Press, 1995.

Webster, John. *Confronted by Grace: Pastoral Meditations from a Systematic Theologian*. Bellingham, WA: Lexham, 2015.

Weil, Simone. "Draft for a Statement of Human Obligations." In *Selected Essays 1934–1943*. London: Oxford University Press, 1962.

―――. *Gravity and Grace*. London: Routledge Classics, 2002.

Williams, Rowan. *Christ on Trial: How the Gospel Unsettles Our Judgment*. Grand Rapids: Eerdmans, 2003.

―――. *Holy Living: The Christian Tradition for Today*. London: Bloomsbury, 2017.

―――. *A Ray of Darkness*. Lanham, MD: Cowley, 1995.

―――. *The Wound of Knowledge*. Lanham, MD: Cowley, 2003.

Wright, Franz. *Ill Lit: Selected & New Poems*. Oberlin, 1998.